BRISTOWS,
10 LIN...
LONDON WC2A 3BP
SOLICITORS:

EUROPEAN LITIGATION HANDBOOK

AUSTRALIA
The Law Book Company
Brisbane • Sydney • Melbourne • Perth

CANADA
Ottawa • Toronto • Calgary • Montreal • Vancouver

AGENTS
Steimatzky's Agency Ltd, Tel Aviv;
N.M. Tripathi (Private) Ltd, Bombay;
Eastern Law House (Private) Ltd, Calcutta;
M.P.P. House, Bangalore;
Universal Book Traders, Delhi;
Aditya Books, Delhi;
MacMillan Shuppan KK, Tokyo;
Pakistan Law House, Karachi, Lahore

EUROPEAN LITIGATION HANDBOOK

By

Tim Taylor
Solicitor, SJ Berwin

and

Nigel Cooper
of Lincoln's Inn, Barrister

LONDON
SWEET & MAXWELL
1995

Published in 1995 by
Sweet & Maxwell Limited of
South Quay Plaza, 183 Marsh Wall, London E14 9FT
Computerset by P.B. Computer Typesetting, N. Yorks
Printed in England by Clays Ltd, St Ives plc

A CIP catalogue record
for this book is available
from the British Library

ISBN 0 421 520809

All rights reserved. UK statutory material in this publication is acknowledged as Crown copyright.
No part of this publication may be reproduced or transmitted in any form or by any means, or stored in any retrieval system of any nature without prior written permission, except for permitted fair dealing under the Copyright, Designs and Patents Act 1988, or in accordance with the terms of a licence issued by the Copyright Licensing Agency in respect of photocopying and/or reprographic reproduction. Application for permission for other use of copyright material including permission to reproduce extracts in other published works shall be made to the publishers. Full acknowledgment of author, publisher and source must be given.

No natural forests were destroyed to make this product, only farmed timber was used and re-planted

©
S.J. Berwin & Nigel Cooper
1995

INTRODUCTION

As Europe, in its widest sense, moves towards closer political and economic ties, so enterprises look to expand into new markets and cross-border ventures. A consequence of these moves is the enhanced risk of litigation spanning one or more jurisdictions. The additional burdens this risk can impose on enterprises and their advisers are many. This handbook, however, only seeks to address itself to one, namely the need to have a basic knowledge of the procedures and remedies available in the various jurisdictions. With this in mind we hope that this book will be of interest to legal practitioners and their clients both in the United Kingdom and abroad.

One of the most difficult decisions we had to make was as to the scope of this book. In the end we decided to limit the jurisdictions we would cover to those of the contracting States to the 1968 Brussels Convention on the Jurisdiction and Enforcement of Judgments in Civil and Commercial Matters and the 1988 Lugano Convention on Jurisdiction and the Enforcement of Judgments in Civil and Commercial Matters. We believe that the implementation of the Conventions and the legal systems of the States party to them are the topics most likely to concern practitioners dealing with cross-border litigation within Europe. The Handbook does cover the legal systems of all the Member States of the European Union and of the Member States of the European Free Trade Association who are party to the Lugano Convention.

The raw material for this handbook was kindly supplied by firms resident in each of the contracting States whose systems are analysed. Acknowledgment of their contribution is set out separately. The scheme of this handbook has flowed naturally from that material. Each Chapter covers a separate issue of jurisdiction, procedure, evidence and enforcement and examines the situation in each contracting State.

It is clear that a work such as this cannot pursue every facet of litigation within the various jurisdictions. We seek only to introduce the systems of the various jurisdictions, to comment upon the impact of the Brussels and Lugano Conventions and to highlight the outstanding areas of exorbitant jurisdiction. Even in these areas this handbook can be only an introductory guide to potential problems. It is not a substitute for the more extensive reference works or for specific legal advice in relation to a particular problem. It follows that we cannot accept any responsibility whatsoever for any consequences arising from reliance on the contents of this handbook.

Nevertheless we hope that this guide will fulfil its initial aims, namely to be an immediate and succinct reference point from which to determine the options and problems that should be pursued further.

We would of course welcome any constructive criticism and comment on this work.

September 1995   *Tim Taylor*
                                                                      Nigel Cooper.

ACKNOWLEDGMENTS

This Handbook would not exist without the support of S.J. Berwin & Co., Solicitors and without the efforts of our colleagues who have so generously contributed the materials that have enabled this work to cover a full 17 jurisdictions. We extend our grateful thanks to these firms for their work and support and for the efforts of our individual colleagues within them.

We are also deeply indebted to Erica Neustadt, of S.J. Berwin & Co., who has provided invaluable assistance in bringing together in a unified format the various contributions upon which the work is based and who has shown an inordinate degree of patience when co-ordinating the production of the final form of the manuscript. For the same degree of patience and for their support, we must also thank our publishers, Sweet & Maxwell.

England
S.J. Berwin & Co.
Tel: 00 44 171 837 2222
Fax: 00 44 171 837 286

Austria
Weiss-Tessbach
Tel: 00 431 533 16 51 140
Fax: 00 431 533 52 52

Belgium
Hanotiau, Evrard & Bruyns & Associes
Tel: 00 32 2 640 35 25
Fax: 00 32 2 648 50 86

Denmark
Arendorff & Partners A/S
Tel: 00 45 33 91 00 60
Fax: 00 45 33 91 03 46

Finland
Procopé & Hornborg
Tel: 00 358 0 694 4466
Fax: 00 358 0 694 8651

Italy
Pavia Ansaldo e Verusio
Tel: 00 39 2 63381
Fax: 00 39 2 2810 0308

Luxembourg
Bonn & Schmitt
Tel: 00 352 455 858
Fax: 00 352 455 859

The Netherlands
Barents & Krans
Tel: 00 31 70 376 0606
Fax: 00 31 70 365 1856

Norway
Thommessen Krefting Greve Lund AS
Tel: 00 47 22 42 18 10
Fax: 00 47 22 42 35 57

Scotland
Morton Fraser Milligan
Tel: 0131 556 8444
Fax: 0131 557 3778

France
Salans Hertzfeld & Heilbronn
Tel: 00 331 4268 4800
Fax: 00 331 4268 1545

Germany
Weiss & Hasche
Tel: 00 49 89 23 80 70
Fax: 00 49 89 23 80 71 10

Greece
Theo V Sioufas Law Offices
Tel: 00 30 1 422 1210
Fax: 00 30 1 422 5090

Ireland
A & L Goodbody
Tel: 00 353 1 661 33 11
Fax: 00 353 1 661 32 78

Spain
Gomez-Acebo & Pombo
Tel: 00 34 1 582 81 00
Fax: 00 34 1 345 36 79

Sweden
Advokatfirman Vinge KB
Tel: 00 46 31 80 51 00
Fax: 00 46 31 15 88 11

Switzerland
Henrici, Wicki & Guggisberg
Tel: 00 41 1 251 66 55
Fax: 00 41 1 252 59 84

CONTENTS

Introduction   v
Acknowledgments   vii

1. The Brussels and Lugano Conventions   1
2. The Court Structure for Civil and Commercial Matters   13
3. The Forms of Originating Process for Civil Litigation   33
4. Conduct of the Proceedings and Pre Trial Preparation   47
5. Interim Protection of Assets Pending Trial   73
6. The Establishment of Jurisdiction   97
7. The Notion of Domicile   115
8. The Service of Foreign Originating Process   125
9. Security for Costs   133
10. The Recognition and Enforcement of Judgments throughout the Contracting States to the Brussels Convention and the Lugano Convention   141
11. The Enforcement and Execution of Judgments   163

Glossary   185
Index   195

CHAPTER 1

THE BRUSSELS AND LUGANO CONVENTIONS

THE APPLICATION OF THE BRUSSELS AND LUGANO CONVENTIONS

1.01. Introduction. The unifying theme of this handbook is provided by the 1968 Brussels Convention on Jurisdiction and the Enforcement of Judgments in Civil and Commercial Matters and the 1988 Lugano Convention on Jurisdiction and the Enforcement of Judgments in Civil and Commercial Matters. In order to understand the relevance of the procedures in the individual States discussed in the following chapters, it is necessary to appreciate the basic framework which the Conventions provide, and which applies to all the jurisdictions we review.

1.02. The Scheme and Scope of the Conventions. The Conventions set out to simplify the reciprocal recognition and enforcement of judgments in the contracting States which make up the European Union and the European Free Trade Association by providing a common regime for the international jurisdiction of the courts of contracting States and a uniform procedure to authenticate and enforce their judgments.

The Conventions apply to all civil matters with specified exceptions[1], of which the most important in a commercial context are insolvency and arbitration.

Note
1. The remaining exclusions are revenue, customs, administrative matters, legal status, rights in matrimonial property, wills and succession and social security.

1.03. Basic Jurisdiction. The starting point of the Conventions is that anyone in a contracting State, whatever their nationality, should be sued in the state where they are based: "domiciled" is

1

the expression used by the Conventions and we consider its technical meaning in Chapter 7.

1.04. Alternatives and Exceptions to Basic Jurisdiction. The Conventions go on to provide for exceptions and alternatives to the basic rule that parties should be sued where they are based. These alternatives and exceptions may be divided into four categories.

1.04:1. Special Jurisdiction. Where the subject matter of particular disputes combines with circumstances that connect them to a State other than the one where the defendant is domiciled, the Conventions permit (but do not require) departure from the basic rule by allowing a domiciliary in a contracting State to be sued, *inter alia*:

(1) in matters relating to a contract, in the courts of the place of performance of the obligation in question;
(2) in matters relating to tort or delict (forms of civil wrong outside a contractual relationship), in the courts for the place where the harmful event occurred, (this may either be where the act or event complained of occurred or where the damage flowing from it was sustained);
(3) in Trust matters, in the courts of the State in which the trust is domiciled[1];
(4) where it is necessary to join a party as an additional defendant or third party to proceedings, in the court where the proceedings against the original defendant are pending.

1.04:2. Exclusive Jurisdiction. The Conventions identify particular subject matters which dictate that the courts of a particular State are the obvious place for the resolution of disputes concerning them.

These subject matters are:

(1) rights in and tenancies of land;
(2) the validity of the constitutions and decisions of companies or other legal persons or their dissolution;
(3) entries in public registers;
(4) the registration or validity of patents or other registrable industrial property rights.

Jurisdiction for proceedings on the above subjects is given exclusively to the State where the land, legal person or register is situated.

1.04:3. Jurisdiction by Agreement. Where parties to a contract have agreed on the court which they wish to rule on any disputes between them, the Conventions normally give effect to their agreement in that respect. Consequently courts apart from the ones chosen by the parties must decline jurisdiction.

1.04:4. Consumer Contracts and Insurance Claims. Policy holders and consumers are given special treatment by the Conventions so that, in almost all circumstances, they must be sued where they are domiciled even though the provisions for special jurisdiction might otherwise allow them to be sued elsewhere.

Note
1. Special provision is also made for maintenance, freight, salvage and the operations of branches and agencies of organisations.

1.05. Ancillary Measures. The Conventions preserve the ability to take ancillary proceedings for provisional measures, for example, to protect assets where they are located, even though the courts of a contracting State elsewhere are the forum for the main proceedings between the parties.

It is important to note that because special jurisdiction under the Conventions is permissive but not mandatory, it will be up to local procedural rules in each of the jurisdictions whether a plaintiff can in fact take advantage of the provisions. That which is permitted by the Conventions is not necessarily permitted by the local rules. Conversely, the long arm jurisdiction under local rules may still permit domiciliaries of non-contracting States to be brought before local courts where the Conventions would preclude the application of those local rules to a domiciliary of a contracting State. The local rules over which the scheme of the Conventions is superimposed are considered in Chapter 6.

1.06. Recognition and Enforcement of Judgments. Together with the rules to provide for the distribution of jurisdiction throughout the contracting States, the Conventions also seek to harmonise the procedures in the various states for the recognition and enforcement of judgments from other contracting States. While the Conventions do not affect the methods of enforcement available in any State, they do limit and define the grounds upon which courts may refuse the recognition or enforcement of a judgment from another contracting State. This topic is covered more fully in Chapter 10.

1.07. Interpretation of the Conventions. The process of harmonisation inherent in the Conventions would founder if there were no possibility for enabling their uniform interpretation among the courts of the contracting States. To this end a power of interpretation over questions arising under the Brussels Convention was originally conferred on the European Court of Justice (the "ECJ"), the original judicial organ of the European Communities.[1] The EFTA States would not have accepted the jurisdiction of the ECJ to give rulings on the Lugano Convention. The Lugano Convention therefore has a different procedure to ensure its uniform application. Protocol 2 on the Uniform Interpretation of the Lugano Convention provides for the courts of each contracting State to pay due regard to the principles laid down by courts of other contracting States when applying the Lugano Convention. The Protocol further sets up a system for consultation and the exchange of information between the contracting States. The object of this system is to collate information at the ECJ on the decisions of national courts and the ECJ which have been delivered pursuant to the Conventions and to exchange information on the working of the Lugano Convention. The contracting States have also signed two Declarations; one by the member States of the European Communities stating that they consider it appropriate that the ECJ should, when interpreting the Brussels Convention, pay due account to rulings on the Lugano Convention, and one by the member States of EFTA that their national courts should, when interpreting the Lugano Convention, pay due account to the rulings of the ECJ and to the national courts of the European Communities on those provisions of the Brussels Convention which are substantially reproduced in the Lugano Convention.

The ECJ was established as the judicial institution of the European Communities to ensure the observance of the law in the interpretation and application of the E.C. treaties. The ECJ's original power of interpretation under the Brussels Convention was granted by way of a 1971 Protocol on Interpretation. This Protocol has been amended to take account of subsequent accessions to the regime of the Brussels Convention. The power of interpretation is exercised by way of preliminary ruling in a manner similar to that under Article 177 of the E.U. Treaty. In summary the procedure allows a national court to refer for preliminary ruling any questions of interpretation under the Brussels Convention which arise in an action being heard by that court. The action before the national court will be stayed pending the preliminary ruling. Once an answer is received from the ECJ, the action before the national court will continue and the national court will apply the ECJ's response to the facts of the action. However, the 1971 Protocol limits to a greater extent than Article 177 the courts which are entitled to request a preliminary ruling from the ECJ. Notably, it excludes the right of courts of first instance to request a preliminary ruling. A court of final instance is bound to refer a question to the ECJ if it considers that a decision on the question is necessary to enable it to give judgment. Any other court having the power to seek a preliminary ruling from the ECJ may seek a reference if it considers that a decision on the question is necessary to enable it to give judgment.

The procedure before the ECJ on a preliminary ruling is similar to that for a reference under Article 177. It is the national court which makes an order for a reference to the ECJ. When the order reaches the ECJ, the Registrar of the Court will send copies to the parties in the national proceedings, to the contracting States, to the Commission and possibly the Council. These are the persons entitled to submit written observations to the Court and to attend the oral hearing. Written observations must be submitted within two months of notification. After any oral submissions by the parties, the Advocate General presents his opinion. Thereafter the ECJ will give its judgment. Costs of the reference will be a decision for the national court.

The 1971 Protocol also provides a power for the competent authorities of contracting States to seek a consultative ruling on interpretation from the ECJ. A consultative ruling may be sought in any case where it appears a judgment of the courts of one contracting State conflicts with the interpretation given by the ECJ or in a judgment of a competent court of another contracting State. The power to seek a consultative ruling only applies in respect of judgments which have been finally and conclusively decided. The competent authorities for this purpose are the Procurators-General of the Courts of Cassation of the contracting State or any other authority designated by a contracting State.

The interpretative jurisdiction of the ECJ has already played a significant role in minimising the differences in application of the Brussels Convention between the courts of the various contracting States. This follows not only from the individual decisions of the ECJ but through their subsequent application as precedent by national courts. As the number of parties to the Brussels Convention and related instruments increases, so will the value of the ECJ's interpretative authority.

Note
1. For further reading on the powers of the ECJ and the court of first instance, see Vaughan, *Law of the European Communities*, Part 2, and Butterworths *Guide to European Court Practice*.

IMPLEMENTATION OF THE CONVENTIONS

1.08. Introduction. In this chapter, we consider the way in which the Conventions have been brought into force in the law of each of the contracting States reviewed.

1.09. United Kingdom. The United Kingdom acceded to the Brussels Convention together with the Republic of Ireland and Denmark by their signature of an Accession Convention dated October 9, 1978. It was given effect in the domestic laws of the United Kingdom by the Civil Jurisdiction and Judgments Act 1982 which was amended to take account of changes introduced by subsequent accession conventions. The United Kingdom ratified the Lugano Convention on February 5, 1992. It was given effect in the United Kingdom by the Civil Jurisdiction and Judgments Act 1991 which amended the 1982 Act and brought the Convention into force in the United Kingdom from May 1, 1992.

1.10. Austria. At the time of writing, the Brussels and Lugano Conventions have not been ratified in Austria, hence its provisions are not applicable as part of the law of the country. Since Austria joined the European Union on January 1, 1995 it has undertaken the obligation to start negotiations on the accession to the Brussels Convention.

1.11. Belgium. The Belgian legislature approved the Brussels Convention by a Statute dated January 13, 1971. It came into force on February 1, 1973 and was amended to take account of modifications following subsequent accessions. The Lugano Convention has not yet been approved.

1.12. Denmark. The Brussels Convention took effect in Denmark partly through Article 247 of the Law on Civil Procedure and partly through the Act on the EEC Convention, Act No. 325 of June 4, 1986. The Convention Act came into force in relation to the original six Member States on November 1, 1986. By Order, the Act entered into force in relation to Great Britain and Northern Ireland from January 1, 1987 and in respect of the Republic of Ireland from June 1, 1988.

Article 1 of the Convention Act incorporates the Brussels Convention as a whole into Danish domestic law. The Law on Civil Procedure provides that the Convention's rules regarding venue shall be applied within the scope of the Convention and provides supplementary rules and regulations.

The Law on Civil Procedure and the Convention do not apply for the Faroe Islands and Greenland.

The Lugano Convention has not yet been ratified by Denmark. However, on March 22, 1995 the Danish Parliament adopted an Act which provides for the ratification of the Convention which the Ministry for Justice expects to enter into force for Denmark within the next six months.

1.13. Finland. The Lugano Convention was approved in Finland by a special Act No. 612 of April 16, 1993. The document of ratification was deposited with the Federal Council of Switzerland on April 27, 1993 and the Convention entered into force on July 1, 1993.

1.14. France. The Brussels Convention was published by Decree no. 73–63 on January 13, 1973. It came into effect on February 1, 1973, three months after ratification. The Lugano Convention was published by Decree no. 92–111 on February 3, 1992. It came into effect on January 1, 1992.

In France, treaties enjoy an authority superior to national law in so far as other contracting parties grant similar treatment under the treaty in question. It is, however, unclear how far the requirement of reciprocal treatment is legitimate. Both the Cours de Cassation and the Conseil d'Etat have refused to verify this condition.

Until recently it was unclear how far treaties took precedence over later contradictory national legislation. This question appears now to have been resolved and both the Cours de Cassation and the Conseil d'Etat have ceded the supremacy of rules of law created by treaty.

1.15. Germany. The original version of the Brussels Convention came into force in the Federal Republic on February 1, 1973. The version as amended in 1978 entered into force on the November 1, 1986. The German legislature passed a law which provided that the provisions of the Convention were automatically included in the body of German law. The so-called Act for the Implementation of Recognition and Enforcement (Anerkennungsund Vollstreckungsausführungsgesetz ("AVAG") was passed to take effect at the same time as the Brussels Convention. This Act contains supplemental rules to the Convention, in particular, the essential ancillary procedural rules.

The Instrument of Ratification for the Lugano Convention was deposited by Germany on December 14, 1994 and came into force on March 1, 1995. The Act for the Implementation of Recognition and Enforcement mentioned above was amended by a law dated September 30, 1994 to include the Lugano Convention.

1.16. Greece. The Brussels Convention as amended became part of Greek domestic law from the April 1, 1989. Greece acceded to the European Conventions generally by the execution of an Accession Treaty in 1979. The Brussels Convention was subsequently ratified and became domestic law by virtue of Law 1814/1988. The formal document of ratification was deposited with the E.C. on January 19, 1989. The Brussels Convention became effective in Greece on the April 1, 1989. Although Greece has signed the Lugano Convention, it has yet to be ratified and therefore does not apply in Greece.

1.17. Ireland. Ireland deposited the Brussels Convention as amended in 1978 in Brussels for ratification in March 1988. Ratification required domestic legislation. The authority was granted by the Jurisdiction of Courts and Enforcement of Judgments (European Communities) Act, 1988. In accordance with the pertinent statutory instrument the Act entered into force on the June 1, 1988.

Under section 3 of the 1988 Act the Brussels Conventions were given the force of law in Ireland and judicial notice shall be taken of it. Further under section 4 of the Act, judicial notice has to be taken of:

(1) any ruling or decision of, or expression of opinion by the European Court on any question as to the meaning or effect of any provision of the Conventions; and
(2) the Jenard, Schlosser and Evrigenis/Kerameus reports.

The San Sebastian Convention and the Lugano Convention have both been ratified by Ireland. The domestic legislation providing the authority for ratification was the Jurisdiction of Courts and Enforcement of Judgments Act 1993 which came into force on December 1, 1993.

1.18. Italy. The Brussels Convention was given effect by Act No. 804, June 21, 1971, published in the Official Gazette of the Republic of Italy, issue 254, October 8, 1971. At the same time the Italian Parliament authorised ratification of the Brussels Convention, which took place on August 10, 1972. The Brussels Convention had the force of law from February 1, 1973. The subsequent accession of the United Kingdom, Denmark and the Republic of Ireland took effect in Italy on November 1, 1985. The Lugano Convention was ratified by Italy by Act 198 of February 10, 1992 and came into force on December 1, 1992.

1.19. Luxembourg. The original Brussels Convention entered the domestic law under a statute dated August 8, 1972. The subsequent Accession Convention of October 9, 1978 was enacted under a law of June 18, 1981. This entered into force on November 1, 1986. The Lugano Convention was ratified and came into force in Luxembourg on July 31, 1991.

1.20. The Netherlands. Under the terms of the Dutch Constitution treaties require parliamentary approval. The Brussels Convention was indorsed by the statute of May 4, 1972. Consequently the Brussels Convention was ratified on June 26, 1972 to come into force on February 1, 1973. The Lugano Convention was ratified on January 23, 1990 and came into force on January 1, 1992.

1.21. Norway. Norway acceded to the Lugano Convention and the Convention was given effect through the Act for the Implementation of the Lugano Convention, January 8, 1993 No. 21. By Royal Decree, the Act entered into full force in Norway from May 1, 1993. According to Article 1 of the Act the Lugano Convention as a whole is incorporated into Norwegian domestic law. The changes required to harmonise Norwegian law with the Convention were made to the Norwegian Civil Procedure Act 1915 and other relevant Acts with effect from May 1, 1993.

1.22. Portugal. Portugal signed the San Sebastian Convention on May 26, 1989. Under the terms of that Convention, she acceded to the Brussels Convention. The Treaty came into force when it was approved by the Parliament and ratified by the President of the Republic. Both the Brussels and Lugano Conventions were ratified on October 30, 1991 and came into force on July 12, 1992.

1.23. Spain. Spain acceded to the Brussels Convention, as well as to the Protocol regarding its construction by the Court of Justice of the Community (Luxembourg, June 3, 1971) by the San Sebastian Convention, May 26, 1989, ratified by the Ministry of Justice, on behalf of the Crown, on October 29, 1990. It was enacted on February 1, 1991 following its official publication on January 28, 1991. The Lugano Convention was enacted on November 1, 1994 following its ratification on August 9, 1994.

Pursuant to Article 96 of the Spanish Constitution, validly concluded international treaties become part of internal law, following their official publication in Spain. Their provisions can only be modified, suspended or repealed in accordance with the provisions of the treaties themselves, or with the rules of International Law.

1.24. Sweden. Sweden acceded to the Lugano Convention in 1992 which was given effect in Swedish law from January 1, 1993. The relevant act regarding the accession is SFS 12992:794.

1.25. Switzerland. The Lugano Convention has been ratified by Switzerland on October 18, 1991 and came into effect on January 1, 1992. Its provisions are considered to be part of the

Swiss legal system and are as such directly applicable.

The Lugano Convention, as a Treaty, ranks above the existing federal laws and above all cantonal laws in the Swiss legal hierarchy, i.e. in case of contradictions between a federal or cantonal law and the treaty, the treaty prevails. The relationship between treaties and federal laws which enter into force after the treaty is more complex. However, the question is unlikely to arise in the near future as most procedural laws in Switzerland are cantonal laws.

Switzerland has made a reservation to the Convention in view of Article 59 of the Swiss Constitution which grants every defendant with a domicile in Switzerland the right that personal claims against him have to be brought before the courts of his domicile. The reservation provides for the possibility for the Swiss courts to deny the recognition and enforcement of a foreign judgment if:

(1) the foreign court has based its jurisdiction solely on art. 5 para. 1 of the Convention (jurisdiction at the place of performance of a contract);
(2) and the defendant had his domicile in Switzerland at the time of service of foreign originating process;
(3) and the defendant objects to the recognition and enforcement of the foreign judgment in Switzerland.

The reservation is limited until December 31, 1999.

CHAPTER 2

THE COURT STRUCTURE FOR CIVIL AND COMMERCIAL MATTERS

2.01. Introduction. The network of courts within each European country is broadly divided by region, subject matter and financial limits, overlaid by a hierarchy for appeal.

Commonly, regional courts deal with smaller disputes and those modern states born of unification such as Italy, Spain and Germany retain a legacy of local courts whose geographical jurisdiction may echo political boundaries now invisible.

Nowadays, financial limits are usually added to the geographical constraints of local courts' jurisdiction with separate higher courts dealing with more substantial litigation. It is also common for the affairs of commercial men to rank for separate treatment from those of other citizens, with special commercial courts established to adjudicate on their disputes.

In commercial matters the great unifying force throughout continental Europe was the codification of the law born of the thinking of the Enlightenment and spread by the endeavours of Napoleon Bonaparte. The main force of this influence stopped with Napoleon at the Channel. This accounts for the schism in the legal world between continental European civil law (originating from Roman Law and set down in written Codes to be interpreted by the courts) and the judge-made common law exported by Britain to its former colonies.

As will be seen, some facets of this historical divide continue to influence the way in which modern litigation is conducted, in particular the roles assumed by advocates and judges in the different systems. Nevertheless it will also be seen that the broad framework of courts in which they operate is structurally quite similar.

2.02. England and Wales. Within England and Wales civil jurisdiction at first instance is divided between the High Court and the County Courts.

Within the High Court civil and commercial matters will tend to fall within the jurisdiction of the Queen's Bench Division, and

14 The Court Structure for Civil and Commercial Matters

particularly the commercial court. Matters concerning the formation of companies and their structure as well as intellectual property questions fall within the ambit of those matters dealt with by the Chancery Division. Allied to these more general jurisdictions the High Court also exercises a specialised Admiralty jurisdiction.

The commercial court was established in 1895 to provide a tribunal with a greater understanding and acquaintance with commercial and business disputes. Its procedures are designed to ensure the swift resolution of litigation without such formalities as may be unnecessary where the litigants are generally business people. Given the great importance which interlocutory applications may have in commercial litigation, all such applications are dealt with by judges (rather than masters). Practitioners before the court are mainly specialists in commercial litigation and there is a great degree of co-operation between the court and practitioners in the conduct and organisation of litigation.

In general, appeal from the judgments of both the High Court and a County Court is to the Court of Appeal, Civil Division. Such appeal can be on matters of fact and law, however appeal courts will only interfere with decisions of the judge at first instance on matters of fact or discretion in very restricted circumstances. Further appeal lies to the House of Lords, but requires the leave of either the Court of Appeal or the Appeal Committee of the House of Lords.

In most civil and commercial matters, the financial value of the case determines the court in which litigation should be commenced. Since the entry into force of the Courts and Legal Services Act 1990 both the High Court and the County Court have unlimited jurisdictions in matters of contract and tort. However, there are rebuttable presumptions that matters with a value below £25,000.00 will be commenced in the County Court and that matters with a value above £50,000.00 will be heard in the High Court. Where the High Court is satisfied that an action is one which should have been commenced in the County Court it will order the transfer of the proceedings. Further if the High Court considers that the person commencing the proceedings knew or ought to have known that they should have been brought in a County Court, it has a power to strike out the proceedings or penalise the person in costs. The County Court has similar powers in respect of proceedings which should have been begun in the High Court.

The County Court generally has the same powers as the High Court in the exercise of its power to grant ancillary relief.

However as from July 1, 1991, the County Court lost its power to grant Mareva Injunctions and Anton Piller Orders, save in limited and exceptional circumstances.

2.03. Scotland. In Scotland, civil jurisdiction at first instance is divided between the Court of Session and the Sheriff Court. There are six different Sheriffdoms, each divided into districts, and in all there are 49 sheriff courts. The Court of Session, which is the supreme court, sits only in Edinburgh. It is divided into an Outer House (court of first instance) and an Inner House (Appeal Court).

The sheriff court has extensive powers and has concurrent jurisdiction with the Court of Session in most types of actions. There is no pecuniary limit on any action for payment or damages in the Sheriff Court. A case begun in the Sheriff Court can be remitted to the Court of Session on cause shown. The Sheriff Court has exclusive jurisdiction in claims up to £1,500, although again cases which in the court's view are not suitable for the Court of Session may be remitted to the Sheriff Court. The Court of Session has exclusive jurisdiction in certain types of action, for example, actions of reduction, judicial review of administrative decisions or winding up of a company with share capital of more than £120,000.

In general, cases of difficulty are raised in the Court of Session. There is no particular financial rule of thumb as to which court to use. Other considerations may apply: for example, the Court of Session alone can grant warrant to inhibit on the dependence (see Chapter 11) which may justify an otherwise straight forward action being raised there.

One advantage of the procedure in the Court of Session is that special rules exist for the expeditious treatment of commercial causes. A definition is given of a commercial action but the rules are intended to relate to the ordinary transactions of merchants, traders and providers of financial services. The procedure is designed to be attractive to commercial organisations with a view to disposing of the action as soon as possible after it has been raised, ideally within a matter of months. Any action can be raised as a commercial action although the court may convert an action which is unsuitable for the procedure into an ordinary action. Conversely, an action begun as an ordinary action may on the motion of either party be converted into a commercial action. Certain judges are designated as commercial judges.

An appeal lies from the sheriff either to the Sheriff Principal (who presides over the Sheriffdom) and from there to the Inner

House of the Court of Session or alternatively to the Inner House direct. Cases begun in the Court of Session are also appealed to the Inner House. An appeal lies from the Inner House, without leave, to the House of Lords sitting as a Scottish Court.

2.04. Austria. With a few specific exceptions, jurisdiction in all civil proceedings is exercised by a tiered-system of District Courts (Bezirksgericht), district commercial courts (Bezirksgericht für Handelssachen), regional courts (Landesgericht), commercial courts (Handelsgericht), Courts of Appeal (Oberlandesgericht), and the Supreme Court of Justice (Oberster Gerichtshof). Civil claims resulting from criminal offences can, in certain circumstances, be settled during the criminal proceedings.

All first instance disputes regarding money or claims with a monetary value up to AS 100.000, are settled by the district courts, including where appropriate the district commercial courts. These courts also have a wider general jurisdiction including matters such as paternity, maintenance, legitimacy, family law, and boundaries.

All other disputes are handled by regional courts, including, where appropriate, the commercial courts. The regional courts will deal with all disputes arising from employment relationships and there is a separate Labour and Welfare Tribunal (Arbeits- und Sozialgericht) in Vienna. The regional courts exercise appellate jurisdiction over decisions of the district courts.

Appeals from the regional court are to the relevant Court of Appeal.

There is a possible right of appeal against a decision made by the Court of Appeal to the Supreme Court of Justice provided the value of the dispute is over AS 50,000.00. The right of appeal is limited to cases which raise an issue of law having a substantial impact on the maintenance of legal certainty, on law and order or on questions of jurisdiction. For example, there would be a right of appeal where the Court of Appeal has refused to follow a previous judgment of the Supreme Court of Justice or where the issue raised has not been fully considered by the Supreme Court of Justice.

Normally, leave to appeal must be obtained from the Court of Appeal. However, exceptionally the Supreme Court of Justice can be approached directly for leave (Extraordinary appeals).

Commercial disputes are brought before the commercial court or, in smaller matters, the district court for commercial matters. In cases before the commercial court or before the Court of

The Court Structure for Civil and Commercial Matters 17

Appeal on appeal from the commercial court, the tribunal will include one lay assessor from the field of commerce.

Legal representation is compulsory for all claims involving amounts greater than AS 30,000.00. Austrian lawyers have rights of audience in front of all domestic courts and authorities.

2.05. Belgium. Jurisdiction at the lowest level rests with the Justices of Peace (Justice de Paix/Vredegerecht) organised within 225 judicial "cantons". Otherwise, first instance jurisdiction is vested in the Court of First Instance (Tribunal de Première Instance/Rechtbank van Eerste Aanslag) and the commercial court (Tribunal de Commerce/Rechtbank van Koophandel) sitting in 27 "arrondissements".

The division of jurisdiction between the Justices of the Peace and the Courts of First Instance/commercial courts is primarily a financial one. The Justices of the Peace have a general jurisdiction limited to 75,000.00 BF. In addition the Justices of the Peace have exclusive jurisdiction over a number of specifically listed legal matters, in particular landlord and tenant litigation. Jurisdiction between the Court of First Instance and the commercial court depends primarily on the nature of the action or the status of the person against whom it is brought. The Court of First Instance has a general jurisdiction over all civil matters including intellectual property litigation.

The Court of First Instance exercises a criminal jurisdiction as well. In this capacity it has the power to hear civil actions arising out of criminal offences.

The commercial courts have jurisdiction over all cases between businessmen, commercial companies, and commercial partnerships. Private individuals seeking relief against businessmen, companies and partnerships (persons whose acts are presumed to be of a commercial nature unless the contrary is proved) should also bring their case in these courts.

Appeal from the Justices of the Peace is to the Court of First Instance or the commercial court, depending upon the nature of the case.

Appeal from the first instance decisions of the Court of First Instance and the commercial court must go to one of the five Courts of Appeal (Cour d'Appel/Hof van Beroep) established in Brussels, Antwerp, Gent, Mons and Liege.

There is, however, no right of appeal from the Justice of the Peace if the sum at stake is less than 50,000 BF nor from the Court of First Instance or the commercial court if the sum at stake is less than 75,000 BF.

Employment disputes are brought before the Labour Tribunals (Tribunal du Travail/Arbeidsrechtbank), from which appeal lies to the five Labour Courts (Cours du Travail) sitting in the five cities mentioned above.

Every court decision may be challenged before the Supreme Court (Cour de Cassation/Hof van Cassatie). The Supreme Court is comprised of three Chambers, one for civil and tax matters, one for criminal cases and one for employment disputes. Cases brought before the Supreme Court are only reviewed on points of law. Where a decision is declared void, it will be remitted to another court for a fresh hearing on the merits.

Decisions of public authorities can in principle be challenged before the State Council (Conseil d'Etat/Raad van State).

2.06. Denmark. Denmark is divided into 83 judicial districts, each one of which has a district court (byret). The High Court of Denmark (landsret) comprises two geographic divisions; the Eastern Division and the Western Division. The Eastern Division sits in Copenhagen and is composed of a President and 45 High Court Judges. The Western Division is situate in Viborg and composed of a President and 22 High Court Judges. The High Court is collegiate and must generally sit with at least three judges.

The final Court of Appeal is the Supreme Court (Hojesteret), which sits in Copenhagen and is made up of a President and 14 other Supreme Court Judges. Hearings take place before a bench of no less than five judges and, at the discretion of the President, up to seven judges. Denmark also has a separate Maritime and Commercial court comprising a President, one or more Vice-presidents, a judge and a number of experts with particular knowledge of maritime and commercial matters. While in session, the Court is presided over by the President, a Vice-president or the judge acting as presiding judge and either two or four experts.

Apart from the above courts, there are a number of extraordinary courts and tribunals which have been established, including the labour courts, the rent tribunals and livestock arbitration courts. Such courts are composed of one or more professional judges sitting with expert assessors.

Both the district court and the High Court may sit as Courts of First Instance.

Appeal from the district court is to the High Court. Appeal from the High Court sitting in first instance is to the Supreme Court. Only in exceptional cases will a further appeal be allowed

and then only with the permission of the Minister of Justice.
  The decision as to which court shall sit in the first instance is primarily one of financial limit. At present the dividing line is DKK 500,000.00. Claims below DKK 500,000.00 must go to the District Court. For claims over DKK 500,000.00 both the High Court and the District Court have jurisdiction and both parties are entitled to demand that a case brought before the District Court is transferred to the High Court.
  The District Court does have power to refer cases falling below the DKK 500,000.00 threshold to the High Court if it considers that there is a point of major importance for one of the parties at issue.
  Appeals from the High Court and the Maritime and Commercial court take place freely and directly to the Supreme Court.

2.07. Finland. Finland is divided into 70 judicial districts, each one of which has a district court (käräjäoikeus). The composition of the District Court varies according to the nature of the case. Normally in civil and commercial matters the composition is three judges.
  The judgments of the District Court can be appealed in the Courts of Appeal. At the moment there are six Courts of Appeal in Finland. The Courts of Appeal sit in "divisions" or "sections".
  The highest court in Finland is called the Supreme Court which sits in Helsinki and is composed of a president and at least 15 other Supreme Court Judges. A judgment of any Appeal Court may only be appealed to the Supreme Court with leave from the Supreme Court itself. Leave is granted in approximately 10 per cent of applications.
  In addition to the above general courts, there are several special courts in Finland. These include the Insurance Court, the Labour Court, the Water Rights Courts, the Land Tribunals and the Marketing Practice Court.

2.08. France. Civil and commercial matters fall within the jurisdiction of both the private and the public law courts.
  The structure of the public law courts rises from the Courts of First Instance (Tribunaux Administratifs) to the Courts of Appeal (Cours Administratives d'Appel) and the Supreme Court (Conseil d'Etat).
  For the purposes of this handbook, two types of problem fall within the scope of the public law courts

(1) administrative contracts, being:
   (a) contracts bestowing upon the public party rights not available to a party in a contract governed by private law; or
   (b) contracts delegating public powers to a private party; or
   (c) contracts deemed to be public law; for example, those for the completion of public works or authorising the occupation of a parcel of the public domain.
(2) compensation for torts committed by a public authority in the performance of a public function.

Apart from the above, jurisdiction for civil and commercial matters rests with the private law courts. At first instance the Tribunal d'Instance (TI) hears claims for civil demands under FFr. 30,000.00 and has exclusive jurisdiction over most landlord and tenant litigation. The Tribunal de Grande Instance (TGI) has general jurisdiction over all civil matters as well as patent and trademark litigation. The Tribunal de Grande Instance may also sit as the Tribunal Correctionnel to exercise its criminal capacity. In this form it has jurisdiction over civil actions arising out of criminal actions such as misdemeanours.

For commercial matters suit can also be brought before the Tribunal de Commerce. The jurisdiction of this court extends to all suits between businessmen or companies and partnerships deemed to be of a commercial nature. It is also open to private individuals to bring actions against businessmen before this court. The Tribunal de Commerce is staffed with elected businessmen and not with professional judges.

Appeals from all the first instance courts are heard *de novo* by the regional Courts of Appeal. The exception to this are the decisions of the Tribunal d'Instance, which are not subject to appeal if the amount at stake is less than FFr. 13,000.00.

The supreme arbiter of private law cases is the Court of Cassation. Within the court there are civil, commercial and criminal divisions. These consider decisions of the Courts of Appeal by way of review of those decisions. The Court takes no view on the merits of a case. When a decision of a court is declared void, the matter is assigned to another Court of Appeal for them to hear the case on its merits.

Alongside these courts labour disputes are referred to the Conseil des Prud'hommes. The judges sitting in this court are appointed by employers and employees.

2.09. **Germany.** Responsibility for civil and commercial matters rests primarily with the civil and criminal courts ("ordentliche Gerichte") and the labour courts ("Arbeitsgerichte"). Civil claims by an injured party which arise out of a criminal act can also be pursued within the scope of the criminal proceedings ("Adhäsionsverfahren").

Within the civil jurisdiction a four-tiered court system runs from the Local Courts (Amtsgericht) to the Regional Courts (Landesgericht) and Courts of Appeal (Oberlandesgericht) to the Federal Court of Justice (Bundesgerichtshof/BGH). One exception to this system is in Bavaria, where for certain civil matters jurisdiction rests with the Bavarian State Court of Justice (Bayerische Oberstes Landesgericht) rather than the Courts of Appeal or the Federal Court of Justice.

The Local Courts have jurisdiction over matters with a value of DM 10,000.00 or less and a number of other specifically listed legal fields. The Regional Court for any particular district has jurisdiction for pecuniary claims over DM 10,000.00 or where no pecuniary claim is involved. Commercial matters within the jurisdiction of the Regional Court may also be brought before a commercial chamber with three judges. Two of the judges of this chamber are lay members appointed upon the recommendation of the Chamber for Commerce and Industry; the Chairman is however a professional judge.

Subject to a minimum sum being at issue, currently DM 1,500.00, appeal lies from the decision of both the local and regional courts. The Regional Court hears appeals from the Local Court other than in family or affiliation proceedings. The respective Courts of Appeal hear appeals (Berufungen) from the first instance judgments of the Regional Courts, including the commercial chamber and decisions of the family court (part of the Local Court) in family and affiliation proceedings.

No appeal lies from the decisions of the Regional Courts sitting as an appellate court. Decisions of the Courts of Appeal can be taken to the Federal Court of Justice (Revision). Such appeal requires either leave of that Court or an amount in dispute of over DM 60,000.00. Leave will only be granted when the decision appealed has fundamental legal importance or represents a deviation from the decisions of the Federal Court of Justice or the Common Senate of the Federal Appeal Courts. The Federal Court of Justice has the power to refuse to hear an appeal even if the matter meets the qualifying financial limits when it considers the matter is not of fundamental legal importance.

2.10. Greece. The courts in Greece enjoy a three-fold division: civil courts, criminal courts, and administrative courts. Civil and commercial matters are primarily dealt with by the civil courts (politika dikastiria). However the criminal courts are competent to hear civil claims by the victims of a crime for the mental suffering and distress caused to them, or subject to the observance of certain procedural requirements, claims by such victims of a crime for damages in general.

As in all other systems the civil courts have a hierarchical ranking. This is divided as follows:

(1) the Courts [Justices] of Peace (Eirinodikeia);
(2) Courts of First Instance (Protodikeia) (multi-member or single member);
(3) Courts of Appeal (Efeteia);
(4) the Supreme Court on Civil/Commercial and Criminal (but not Administrative) matters (Areios Pagos).

The Courts of Peace are located in all towns where there is a Court of First Instance as well as in other small or mid-sized towns. The competence of the Courts of Peace is determined either by the value of the object in dispute or by the nature of the dispute. In the latter case the value of the object is immaterial.

The Courts of First Instance sit in the main towns of Greece, mostly in the capitals of prefectures. The single member courts hear cases with a higher monetary value than the Courts of Peace as well as cases involving particular special jurisdictions or special procedures such as labour disputes, or most cases of security measures (injunctions).

The three-member court has a general competence for all matters not allotted to the Courts of Peace or the One-Member divisions. It also acts as an appellate court for the cases decided by the Justices of the Peace.

Greece is divided into 11 appellate regions within which sit 12 Courts of Appeal. The extra court is in Piraeus and falls within the Athens appellate area. The Courts of Appeal have a general jurisdiction for all appellate matters not specifically assigned to another court. All appellate hearings before the Court of Appeal and the Court of First Instance are by way of re-hearing on the basis of the evidence before the court at first instance.

The Areios Pagos is the Supreme Court of Greece in respect of civil/commercial cases and also criminal cases. Hearings are on legal issues only and are not full re-hearings of the facts. The Areios Pagos is divided into four divisions, three of which hear appeals. If an appeal is successful, the case is referred to the so-called Division of Committal for a fresh hearing on the merits.

The Court Structure for Civil and Commercial Matters

2.11. Ireland. The structure of the courts in Ireland is regulated by the Courts (Establishment and Constitution) Act 1961. Within the category of lower courts fall the District Court and the Circuit Court. The superior courts comprise the High Court and the Supreme Court.

Ireland is divided into 23 District Court districts. The District Court has a financial limit of IR£ 5,000.00 as the maximum award for civil matters generally. Together with this jurisdiction the District Court also has particular jurisdiction in areas such as debt collection, family law and licensing. Appeals are to the Circuit Court by way of full re-hearing.

There are eight Circuit Court and High Court circuits in Ireland. For matters of tort and contract the jurisdiction of the circuit courts is limited to IR£ 30,000.00. Unlimited jurisdiction can be conferred upon the court with the consent of both parties. The court also has a wide-ranging jurisdiction in landlord and tenant matters where the rateable value of the property is less than IR£200.00 per annum. For matters within its jurisdiction the Circuit Court can exercise equitable powers, including, *inter alia*, the power to grant injunctions.

In addition to its appellate role in relation to the District Court, the Circuit Court is also the appeal court for a number of tribunals, including the Employment Appeals Tribunal.

An Appeal from the circuit court in civil actions is by way of a full re-hearing before the High Court.

The High Court has an unlimited jurisdiction. Normally sitting in Dublin, the Court will hear personal injury and fatal injury claims in other major centres. The right to a jury trial in personal injury actions was abolished by the Courts Act 1988.

Appeals from the High Court in civil and commercial matters are heard by the Supreme Court. Further the Supreme Court may also determine questions put to it by other courts. Upon a referral from the President of Ireland, the Court may also determine the compatibility of any Bill with the Constitution.

2.12. Italy. Competence for civil and commercial matters in Italy is divided between the Justice of the Peace, the Magistrate, the Tribunal, the Court of Appeal, and the Court of Cassation (Giudice di Pace, Pretore, Tribunale, Corte d'Appello and Corte di Cassazione respectively).

The competence of the various first instance courts is divided initially by financial limit. The Justice of the Peace hears matters worth less than Lit. 5,000,000.00 (Lit. 30,000,000.00 for road accident claims). The Magistrate has jurisdiction up to

Lit. 20,000,000.00 as well as over certain specific matters, including possession proceedings. Above Lit. 20,000,000.00 jurisdiction rests with the Tribunal. The Tribunal also sits as the appellate court for cases heard in the first instance by the Magistrate.

Appeal from the Tribunal lies first to the Court of Appeal, while appeal from the Justice of the Peace on questions of law is to the Court of Cassation. The Court of Cassation is also the ultimate tribunal for appellate decisions of the Tribunal or the Court of Appeal.

The domestic jurisdiction of a first instance court is decided by territorial district and basically depends upon considerations of residence or domicile for natural persons and the location of the registered offices for corporations. Additionally there may be special, optional or exclusive criteria — for example, in cases concerning property, jurisdiction is determined by the location of the property. While the rules governing jurisdiction by matter and amount are mandatory, the parties can waive the territorial jurisdiction by mutual written consent prior to trial.

2.13. Luxembourg. The Grand-Duchy is divided into two judicial areas for first instance jurisdiction. The Justices of the Peace (Justices de Paix) have jurisdiction over civil and commercial cases with a value of less than LUF 200,000.00. Appeal in such matters lies to the District Court. The Justices of the Peace also have jurisdiction over specific areas such as labour law. Appeal in these matters is direct to the Court of Appeal.

The District Court (Tribunal d'Arrondissement) has competence over commercial and civil litigation in excess of LUF 200,000.00 and some reserved areas, such as enforcement of foreign judgments.

The appellate jurisdiction for decisions of the Justices of the Peace is exercised by the district court. There is also a Court of Appeal and a Supreme Court. The competence of the latter goes solely to questions of the legality of judgments and orders.

2.14. The Netherlands. First instance jurisdiction is divided between the Local Courts (Kantongerecht) and the district court (Arrondissementsrechtbank). The Netherlands is divided into 62 kantons each with its own local court. The local courts' jurisdiction has a general financial limit of Dfl. 5,000.00, but they have an unlimited jurisdiction in respect of employment, agency, landlord and tenant, hire purchase and agricultural tenancies. Generally there can be no appeal in matters concerning claims for less than Dfl. 2,500.00. In limited circumstances, there may be a right of appeal to the Hoge Raad (Supreme Court). In all other cases appeal is to the district court.

The district courts have a general first instance jurisdiction save for certain types of cases which are specifically assigned to another court. Decisions of the District Court sitting as an appeal court from the Local Courts are final, although there may be an appeal on a point of law to the Supreme Court. First instance decisions are appealed to one of the five Courts of Appeal (Gerechtshoven).

The Courts of Appeal hear appeals from the district courts within their areas. Within the Court of Appeal in Amsterdam there is a special business chamber (Ondernemingskamer) which is responsible for hearing certain types of corporate dispute. The bench in this chamber is supplemented by two expert lay members.

The Supreme Court hears appeals on points of law only, and only in cases in which no normal appeal is available.

2.15. Norway. In Norway there is a four-tiered court system which moves from the local Conciliation Councils ("forliksrad") to the local courts ("herredsrett" in rural areas and "byrett" in urban areas) to the regional courts ("lagmannsrett") and finally to the Supreme Court ("Hoyesterett").

Each local county has its own Conciliation Council to which most civil and commercial matters will be referred in the first instance. The Councils do not employ any professional judges. The bench is occupied by three laymen and the parties are not represented by their lawyers at hearings. The Councils' main task is to assist the parties to reach an amicable settlement. The Councils' jurisdiction is limited to claims of less than NOK 20,000. Most cases will therefore be referred to the local courts following an initial hearing in the Council.

There are 105 local judicial districts each of which has its own local court. The local courts have jurisdiction over all civil and commercial matters. There is no financial limit to the cases they may hear.

Hearings in the local courts normally take place before a bench of one professional judge. However, at the request of the parties, or on the court's own motion, the bench may include two laymen.

An appeal from a judgment of a local court must be filed within two months to the applicable regional court. There are five regional courts, seated in Oslo, Bergen, Skien, Trondheim and Tromso. The appellant needs the regional court's leave to bring the appeal if the matter relates to an amount of less than NOK 20,000.

Hearings in the regional court take place before a bench of three professional judges. Again, at the request of the parties or on the court's own motion, the bench may also include either two or four laymen.

If there is a further appeal to the Supreme Court, the appeal must be filed within two months. A further appeal may only be submitted if the case involves claims in excess of NOK 100,000, and will always be subject to the approval of the Appeals Division of the Supreme Court ("Hoyesteretts kjoeremalsutvalg").

The Supreme Court is located in Oslo and consists of 18 judges. Hearings in the Supreme Court normally take place before a bench of five Supreme Court Judges.

Only a very limited number of cases involving matters of a constitutional nature will be heard by the Court in a plenary sitting.

Alongside the four-tiered system, there are a number of extraordinary courts and tribunals, for example labour courts, rent tribunals and social security tribunals.

2.16. Portugal. Civil and commercial jurisdiction rests with the civil courts, the Tribunais Civeis. Jurisdiction is divided among the various judicial levels according to matter, hierarchy, value and territory. The court structure moves through three instances; the Courts of First Instance ("de Comarca"), Second Instance ("Relações) and the Supreme Court of Justice. The Courts of First Instance have a general jurisdiction which is without prejudice to the specific jurisdiction of other courts, the most important of which are the commercial courts, the criminal courts, the family courts, the labour courts and the Maritime Courts.

2.17. Spain. The Spanish court structure divides jurisdiction into four broad categories: civil, criminal, administrative and social. Commercial matters are generally dealt with by the courts with civil jurisdiction.

Civil jurisdiction is divided between the Courts of Peace (Juzgados de Paz), Courts of First Instance (Juzgados de Primera Instancia), Provincial High Courts (Audiencias provincials),

The Court Structure for Civil and Commercial Matters 27

Higher Courts of Justice (Civil Section) (Tribunales Superiores de Justicia, Sala de lo civil) and the Supreme Court (Civil Section) (Tribunal Supremo, Sala de lo civil).

The diversity of courts permits a structure with a duality of instances, and a final appeal by cassation. First instance jurisdiction rests with the Courts of Peace and Courts of First Instance. The former generally deal with claims for amounts lower than 8,000 pesetas. The civil sections of the Supreme Court and High Courts handle claims for liability of public officials and civil servants at first instance.

Appeals filed against decisions by the Courts of Peace are heard by the Courts of First Instance. Appeals filed against decisions taken by the Courts of First Instance are resolved by the Provincial High Courts (Second Instance). Depending on the case, the Civil Sections of the Higher Courts of Justice and the Supreme Court decide appeals on points of law.

There are 17 Higher Courts of Justice (one for each Region), 51 Provincial High Courts (one per Province), one Court of First Instance for each court district (in larger cities, there is more than one such district) and one Court of Peace per township if it has no Court of First Instance.

The jurisdiction of a specific court within the Spanish territory is determined following a set of criteria known as "fueros". The determining criterion is the express or implicit submission of the parties to a particular court.

Alternatively, where there is no such submission, the jurisdiction of a particular court is determined by the operation of law, which provides for 27 special rules and for general criteria applicable to cases to which these rules do not apply. For example, in actions "in rem", the plaintiff has the choice between taking action where the property in dispute is located and where the defendant lives. In actions "in personam", the plaintiff should take action through the court where the parties' obligations should have been performed. If this cannot be established then the plaintiff has the choice between taking action where the cause of action arose and where the defendant lives.

In general the plaintiff will take action in the court which has jurisdiction over the place where the defendant lives.

2.18. **Sweden.** The Swedish court is a three-tiered system:

(1) the District Court (tingsrätt),
(2) the Court of Appeal (hovrätt), and
(3) the Supreme Court (Högsta Domstolen).

Sweden is divided into 97 judicial districts, each of which has its own District Court. All civil and commercial matters come under the jurisdiction of these courts at first instance. There are no financial limits for the commencement of proceedings before the District Courts.

Hearings in the District Courts take place before one or three professional judges. The number depends mainly upon the complexity of the matter.

In most civil and commercial matters, the appeal of a judgment from a District Court to the Court of Appeal must be filed within three weeks from the date of judgment. There are six Courts of Appeal, each covering a number of District Courts. The Courts of Appeal are situated in Stockholm, Göteborg, Malmö, Jönköping, Sundsvall and Umeå. With the exception of very small matters there are no financial or other restrictions on making appeals in civil matters to the Court of Appeal.

Hearings in the Court of Appeal take place before a bench of three to four professional judges.

The Supreme Court is situated in Stockholm and consists of 22 Justices of the Supreme Court.

An appeal from a Court of Appeal will be tried by the Supreme Court only if the Court grants a hearing ("prövningstillstånd"). Only a limited number of cases are granted such a hearing. The usual reason for a hearing is that the matter is of general importance for the interpretation and application of law.

Hearings in the Supreme Court take place before a bench of three to seven Supreme Court Justices.

2.19. Switzerland. In Switzerland the responsibility for the organisation of the judiciary and for the procedural laws lies with the cantons. Consequently, there are 26 different systems as well as 26 different Codes of Civil Procedure. Although it can be said that the systems are at least similar in the different cantons, it is always advisable to consult local counsel before taking any legal steps. This summary will limit itself to the court structure of the Canton of Zurich which is Switzerland's most important business centre. In the Canton of Zurich civil and commercial jurisdiction at first instance is divided between different local single judges (Einzelrichter) and district courts (Bezirksgerichte), special courts for labour and for lease disputes (Arbeits- und Mietgerichte), the cantonal commercial court (Handelsgericht), and the Cantonal High Court (Obergericht).

Criteria for the division of competence at first instance are, firstly, the nature and type of proceedings (civil/commercial matters, labour/lease disputes, intellectual property litigation; ordinary/summary proceedings) and secondly, or alternatively, the value of the litigation.

2.19:1. Single Judges. Civil claims with a value of SFr. 8,000.00 or less are dealt with by the single judges in ordinary proceedings. The single judges also decide all civil and commercial matters which are to be heard in summary proceedings ("summarisches Verfahren") or accelerated proceedings (beschleunigtes Verfahren). Essentially, such proceedings will relate to debt collection matters, bankruptcy proceedings, and any form of provisional measure when the substantive proceedings have not been commenced. Requests for legal assistance in civil matters fall within the competence of the single judges.

2.19:2. District Courts. The district courts hear civil matters with a value of more than SFr. 8,000.00 or with a value which cannot be measured in money, in ordinary proceedings.

2.19:3. Labour Courts. Disputes between employers and employees based on the employment contract are heard by the special local labour courts (Arbeitsgerichte), unless the parties decide to bring the dispute before the ordinary courts. The labour courts consist of three members, the president who is a judge at the district court and two assessors, one representative of the employer and one representative of the employee.

2.19:4. Lease Courts. Disputes over lease agreements have to be brought before the special local lease courts (Mietgerichte), unless otherwise agreed to by the parties. The lease courts are constituted according to the same pattern as the labour courts (one judge, one representative of the landlords, and one representative of the tenants).

2.19:5. Cantonal Commercial Court. The cantonal commercial court hears matters of a commercial nature and a value of more than SFr. 12,000.00 when both parties are registered as firms in the Swiss commercial register. If only the defendant is registered but otherwise the conditions mentioned above are met, the claimant may choose between the commercial court and the ordinary courts. If the defendant is registered as a firm in a foreign register similar to the Swiss commercial register or is considered to be a businessman under the law of his foreign domicile, and the other conditions mentioned above are met, the claimant may choose between the commercial court and the ordinary courts whether or not he is registered as a firm in the Swiss commercial register. The parties can agree upon the jurisdiction of the commercial court in disputes concerning commercial matters with a value of more than SFr. 12,000.00.

Finally, the commercial court hears disputes concerning certain intellectual property rights, anti-trust matters, and investment funds.

Proceedings before the commercial court do not differ procedurally from those in the ordinary civil court. The difference lies before the composition of the commercial court which consists of high court judges and experienced business people.

2.19:6. Cantonal High Court. The Cantonal High Court sits as a first instance court for copyright disputes. Otherwise, the High Court acts as an appellate court for appeals against decisions of the labour courts, the lease courts and the District Courts in civil matters with a value of more than SFr. 12,000.00 and for decisions of the single judges at the district, labour or lease courts in civil matters of a value of more than SFr. 8,000.00.

2.19:7. Cantonal Court of Cassation. Appeals against decisions of the High Court, the commercial court, as well as of the single judges at those courts are heard by the Court of Cassation (Kassationsgericht). Appeals are limited to questions of law.

2.19:8. Swiss Federal Supreme Court. To ensure a certain uniformity in the application of the federal civil and commercial law the Swiss Federal Supreme Court hears appeals against final cantonal decisions in civil or commercial matters with a value of more than SFr. 12,000.00 or without a value which can be expressed in monetary terms, and in all disputes concerning certain intellectual property rights as well as some other specific matters. As an appellate court, the Federal Supreme Court only deals with questions

The Court Structure for Civil and Commercial Matters

of law and does not review the factual basis of cantonal decisions.

In some specific cases the Federal Supreme Court acts as first instance court (for example, if the value of the litigation is more than SFr. 20,000.00 and both parties agree on the Supreme Court having jurisdiction). In such cases procedure is governed by the Federal Code on Civil Procedure.

CHAPTER 3

THE FORMS OF ORIGINATING PROCESS FOR CIVIL LITIGATION

3.01. Introduction. The first step in any court action, whatever name may be given to it, amounts to a request by the plaintiff to the court to rule upon an issue and the court's consequent command to the defendant to submit to its decision on that request. The means by which this procedure is invoked is termed "Originating Process".

The question that logically precedes any issue as to whether the plaintiff's request has merit is whether the chosen court has the jurisdiction to pronounce a judgment which will bind the protagonists and so be enforced not only in the country where it was pronounced but also elsewhere.

In general a challenge to the court's jurisdiction must be made at the outset before a party enters into any debate on the issue brought before the court. The common scheme adopted by the Conventions to determine whether a domestic court has jurisdiction has already been considered in Chapter 1. The Conventions rely upon the court in which the originating process is issued to operate the rules laid down by the scheme. When the powers of a court elsewhere in the community are invoked to enforce a judgment of the court in which the originating process was issued it will generally be too late to challenge the authority of the original court to deliver the judgment. Thus, if a challenge is not made at the outset, the right to make it at all may be lost altogether. Hence, anyone faced with proceedings in an unfamiliar jurisdiction will need to understand in the first place the form of originating process they may expect to receive and the time in which they may be called upon to respond.

3.02. England and Wales. Proceedings in the High Court are generally begun either by writ or originating summons. The writ is the more usual form of originating process where there is a factual dispute between the parties. An originating summons is more usual in the Chancery Division and is the appropriate form of process for various forms of application or where the issue is purely one of law. That said, the plaintiff has freedom of choice, save that the following must be begun by writ:

(1) actions in tort other than trespass to land;
(2) claims based on fraud;
(3) claims for damages for breach of duty in respect of death, personal injuries or damage to property;
(4) infringements of patents;
(5) admiralty actions in rem;
(6) probate actions.

Proceedings in the County Court are divided into Actions which are begun by Plaint and Matters which are begun by Originating Application or Petition. Actions are divided into Default Actions, claims for money only, and Fixed Date Actions, every other action. Originating Applications are generally used for actions invoking the jurisdiction of a special statute, while Petitions are generally only used for matrimonial matters.

All forms of originating process must identify the parties, provide a statement of the nature of the claim or the questions upon which the plaintiff seeks the determination of the court and state the relief sought. It is sufficient in the first instance that a writ or summons bears only a summary of the claim. A separate "Statement of Claim" setting out the plaintiff's claim and the relief sought in full detail will then either be served with the writ or at a later date.

Proceedings are issued by filing the originating process with the appropriate court office. In the High Court a writ is initially valid for four months from the date of issue (six months, if leave for service out of the jurisdiction is required).

Service of proceedings in the High Court is the responsibility of the plaintiff. Prima facie, the writ must be served personally upon any defendant. However, if the defendant is within the jurisdiction, the writ may be served by ordinary first-class post to the defendant at his usual or last-known address or, if there is a letter-box for that address, by inserting the writ through the letter box in a sealed envelope addressed to the defendant.

Service of proceedings in the County Court is effected by the court itself. On receipt of the papers from the plaintiff, the court will prepare a summons and send this together with a copy of the Particulars of Claim, an Admissions Form and a Defence and Counterclaim Form to the defendant.

In the High Court, once the proceedings have been served upon the defendant he must acknowledge the service of the originating process and either admit the plaintiff's claim or give notice of his intention to defend. Failure to acknowledge service

The Forms of Originating Process for Civil Litigation 35

and give notice of intention to defend, may lead to the plaintiff entering judgment in default against the defendant. A similar procedure is followed in the County Court.

3.03. Scotland. Proceedings in the Court of Session are begun either by Summons or Petition. The latter procedure invokes the administrative jurisdiction of the court and seeks the authority of the court to permit or to require something to be done. The procedure is speedy and flexible. For example, applications for Judicial Review, liquidation under the Companies Act and, on occasion, Interdict are brought by way of Petition. Where there is a contentious issue between parties such as claims for damages, breach of contract, Admiralty actions or for payment, the pursuer begins the procedure by way of Summons.

In the Sheriff Court there is a similar division of procedure although the terminology is different. All actions begun in the Sheriff Court are initiated by an Initial Writ.

In both the Court of Session and the Sheriff Court the action is commenced by a document which must set out in detail the remedies sought, the factual basis justifying the claim and the legal basis on which the alleged facts justify the remedy. The originating document (the Summons, Petition or Initial Writ, depending on the nature of the procedure) is presented to the appropriate court office and the necessary warrant or authority is obtained to serve the writ. It is the responsibility of the pursuer's (plaintiff's) lawyer to arrange for service of the writ and warrant. The writ may be served either personally by a Messenger-at-Arms or by a First Class Recorded Delivery letter. Prescriptive periods (time limits) normally only stop running once the defender has received the writ so it is important to commence proceedings in good time to allow for any problems in securing effective service of the action. Once the defender has received the writ he must take steps usually within 21 days to give notice to the court that he intends to defend although in certain types of procedure (eg Companies Act liquidation) there is a shorter period.

3.04. Austria. Normally actions are begun by writ (Klage). For disputes up to AS 30,000.00, the plaintiff may start the proceedings personally by issuing a court protocol Gerichtsprotokoll. Proceedings for the recovery of a debt up to AS 100,000.00 may be begun by the issue of a summons for recovery of money (Mahnklage). A plaintiff does this by completing a simple court form. Proceedings for the recovery of a debt greater than AS 100,000.00 are begun by writ.

In proceedings begun by "Mahnklage" and in proceedings involving bills of exchange and cheques, the summons is effectively an order to pay. The defendant has 14 days to put in a defence to the summons. In the event that no defence is raised, the summons takes effect as a legally binding order to pay having the same force as a judicial decision. In the event that a defence is entered, the summons becomes the originating process in the action which then continues normally.

Notice of proceedings is served on the opposing party by the court. However, if the defendant cannot be served, the plaintiff is informed and it is his responsibility to trace the defendant's new address or new place of work. If it is impossible to find the defendant's place of residence, the plaintiff can apply to the court for an administrator to be appointed for the defendant. The costs of such an administrator must be temporarily borne by the plaintiff.

3.05. Belgium. Civil actions are usually commenced by means of a summons served by a bailiff. The bailiff is instructed by the lawyer acting on behalf of the plaintiff. Upon receipt of instructions, the bailiff issues the official summons ("exploit de citation").

Service is effected personally. Failing that, it may be made at the domicile of the defendant (or his residence, if he has no domicile) by delivering the summons to a parent, a person related by marriage, an agent or servant. In the absence of such service, notification can be made at the local police station.

Otherwise, in circumstances defined in the Civil Code, litigation can be commenced by *ex-parte* petition (Article 700, Judicial Code), voluntary appearance of the parties before the court (Articles 1025 *et seq.*, Judicial Code) or, for certain statutory proceedings, by written request delivered to the Clerk of the Court for notification to the defendant (Article 704, Judicial Code).

3.06. Denmark. Proceedings are begun by writ (staevning). This must contain certain information, including the name and address of the parties, designation of the court at which proceedings are to be commenced, a statement of claim and the relief sought. In addition the writ must set out the documents and other evidence (including witnesses) upon which the plaintiff intends to rely. Copies of the writ and such documents as are in the plaintiff's possession are filed with the court.

After the court has verified that the writ is in order the writ is indorsed with the date and time of the first hearing. Service is generally effected by the court. Service will primarily be by process server at the domicile of the defendant and must be confirmed by the defendant's signature. Alternatively service may be by post or by delivery.

At the first court hearing the defendant serves his defence. This must contain a statement of defence, any counterclaim and a statement of fact in support as well as a list of any documents or other evidence relied on in support. Before the district court the statement of defence may be given orally. Further pleadings such as a reply and rejoinder may be allowed.

3.07. Finland. Civil actions are initiated by means of a written application for a summons sent to the office of a district court. The application must contain certain information, including the plaintiff's detailed claim and information about evidence that the plaintiff intends to present. When the court has issued a summons, the defendant is invited to respond in writing. The general rule is that service of the summons is the responsibility of the court and is usually served by mail against an acknowledgement of receipt but may also be served by special officials or process servers.

3.08. France. Adversarial proceedings normally begin with the issue of a summons (assignation) prepared by the avocat. It can only be served by a sworn bailiff (huissier de justice) and must be served personally upon the defendant. The defendant must appoint an avocat within fifteen days otherwise default judgment can be entered.

Cases to be heard upon short notice require prior leave of the court for a fixed-date summons. Such summons go by different names before the various tribunals: "assignation à jour fixe" before the Tribunal de Grande Instance, "assignation à bref délai" before the Tribunal de Commerce, "assignation en référé d'heure à heure" before both courts for urgent interlocutory proceedings.

Ex parte proceedings can be instituted by the avocat submitting a request (requête) to the President of the Court. Any order (ordonnances sur requête) then granted is generally entrusted to the bailiffs for enforcement. Service of the order can then be challenged by a summons to appear at short notice and show cause (référé).

Administrative proceedings and individual labour disputes do not require the issue of a summons. Administrative proceedings are commenced by application (recours), including a statement of claim, filed with the Clerk of the Court, who forwards it to the other party.

Individual labour disputes can be initiated by filing at court a form indicating the amount of the dispute and legal reasoning for the claim. The Clerk of the Conseil des Prud'hommes transmits the form to the defendant.

3.09. Germany. An action is generally started by filing a writ with the court. Certified copies must also be filed for each defendant, and where legal representation is compulsory, an additional copy for each defendant. All other necessary copies will be prepared by the court at the expense of the plaintiff. The writ will then be served upon the defendant by the court.

There is no obligation to be legally represented at local courts. Accordingly, the cause of action can be recorded directly at the court. In such a case, the court record will be served upon the defendant rather than the writ.

Ex parte proceedings are possible for judgment on a debt. This allows a plaintiff to obtain executory judgment without actual court proceedings. This form of proceedings may only be used for liquidated sums expressed in domestic currency. Service of the demand for payment is possible in a contracting party to the Conventions. In this case the demand may be expressed in a foreign currency. Appeal against the demand for payment must be lodged within 14 days. Then, the matter will be transferred to adversarial proceedings. If no appeal is lodged in time, a writ of execution may be issued. This writ may also be appealed within 14 days. Under certain circumstances, this appeal may be lodged using other special legal proceedings.

3.10. Greece. A civil or commercial action in Greece is begun by filing the appropriate form of originating process with the competent court. The form is determined by the remedy sought. All forms of originating process are submitted to the secretariat of the court and are signed by the authorised attorney of the plaintiff. Common forms of originating process include:

(1) an Action (Agogi);
(2) a Petition (Aitisis);

(3) Objections (Anakopi or Tritanakopi);
(4) the Direct or Principal Intervention (Kyria Paremvasis);
(5) Ancillary Intervention (Prosthetos Paremvasis);
(6) Notification of Trial (Anakoinosis Dikis);
(7) Third Party Proceedings (Prosepiklisis).

In the case of Actions, Objections, Petitions, and sometimes for Third Party Proceedings, Interventions and Notification of Trial, the defendant must be duly served with a copy of the complaint. Once service has been duly effected, the proceedings are valid from the time they were filed with the court. The duty to serve the defendant rests with the plaintiff and is carried out for defendants resident or domiciled in Greece by a court bailiff for the area of that domicile or residence.

Service on the defendant must be within the time period laid down. Accordingly for Actions, Objections, Third Party Proceedings, Notification of Trial or Principal Intervention, the service must be at least 30 clear days before the hearing fixed by the court; 60 clear days if the defendant is domiciled or resident outside Greece and does not have an agent in Greece authorised to accept service (antikletos).

Where an action is subject to a limitation period, the originating process must have been both filed and served before the expiry of the relevant period.

It should be noted that under the provisions of the Code of Civil Procedure a creditor with a liquidated monetary claim against a person residing in Greece is entitled to apply *ex parte* to the Justice of the single-member Court of First Instance for a payment order which, although not technically a judgment, constitutes an instrument of title for execution (enforcement). Upon service of the payment order, the defendant is entitled to raise objections and also to seek an adjournment of execution.

3.11. Ireland. The appropriate form of originating summons is determined by the relevant rules of court.

Before the district court, actions are commenced by civil process. For contract and tort claims the usual form is the ordinary civil process. Actions for liquidated sums may be commenced by summary civil process.

Proceedings in the circuit court begin with the issue of a civil bill. Debt collection, contract and tort claims are initiated by means of an ordinary civil bill. For possession actions in landlord and tenant claims the correct form of originating process is an ejectment civil bill. Equitable jurisdiction is sought through the issue of an equitable civil bill.

In the High Court proceedings are generally commenced by way of originating summons and less frequently by petition or Originating Notice of Motion. The most common form of summons is the plenary summons, but there are other forms for particular types of action. Actions in respect of debts, liquidated demands and, in certain circumstances, possession of land may be instituted by summary summons. Certain actions, including those for the construction of documents, the determination of wills, certain matters concerning trustees and mortgage suits are commenced by special summons.

3.12. **Italy.** The categories of originating process provided for under Italian law can be divided into three types:

(1) cognizance;
(2) enforcement;
(3) special proceedings.

> 3.12:1. **Cognizance proceedings.** The cognizance procedure covers so-called "actions of inquiry" intended to resolve the dispute between the parties; "actions of conviction" intended to result in the conviction of one or more parties to the proceedings as well as to resolve the legal dispute; and "actions of constitution" which result in an order giving immediate legal effect without the need for later enforcement.
>
> All forms of cognizance procedure are begun by a writ of summons (atto di citazione) issued by the plaintiff, filed with the appropriate court and served on the defendant with a notice to appear before the court. The writ includes the plaintiff's claim, statement of case and the evidence (if any) which the plaintiff is going to submit to support his case.
>
> 3.12:2. **The Enforcement Procedure.** The individual forms of enforcement are discussed more fully in Chapter 11 below. The procedure for enforcement can only be begun on the basis of a "document of title" recognised to be enforceable at law. Such "documents of title" include a court order, bills of exchange, credit instruments or such deeds as may be specified under the law and are certified by a notary public or other authorised court official.

3.12:3. Special Process.

Italian law provides for certain proceedings as exceptions to the ordinary cognizance procedure. These can be divided into special "full" cognizance proceedings and special "summary" cognizance proceedings.

Special "full" cognizance proceedings vary from ordinary cognizance proceedings either by reason of their subject matter or by reason of the urgency of the proceedings. Examples are matters involving labour disputes, questions of appeal against arbitration awards alleged to be void and of appeal against decisions of the Tax Commission.

Although special "summary" cognizance proceedings lead to a judgment on the merits, the examination of the dispute by the court is summary and accordingly not as comprehensive as at full trial. Typical actions of this nature include injunction proceedings, or orders for eviction. If the orders granted in summary proceedings are not challenged by the defendant, they will become final. If, however, the order is challenged ordinary cognizance proceedings must be begun.

3.13. Luxembourg.

Civil or commercial proceedings are initiated by a writ of summons served by a bailiff. For actions begun before the Tribunal Civil or the Tribunal de Commerce the writ is known as an "assignation". Before the Justice of the Peace, the correct title is "citation".

Before the commercial court or the Justice of the Peace the summons requires the defendant to attend the court on a fixed date named therein. For proceedings before the civil court the lawyer for the defendant must give the plaintiff written notice within eight days of service that he represents the defendant's interests

Rent and employment disputes can be begun by filing a request with the court. The secretary of the court then serves notice upon the defendant by post. In bankruptcy cases the commercial court has the power to declare companies and businessmen insolvent without proceedings.

3.14. The Netherlands.

The documentation for beginning proceedings are brief. The summons (dagvaarding) is served upon the defendant together with a certificate of service and a statement of the plaintiff's case, including the relief sought.

Particular forms of proceeding are begun by petition (verzoekschrift). This includes the grounds for claim and again the relief sought. After it is filed at the court, the court clerk sends a copy to the respondent. A defence may be filed, but there are no other pleadings.

In proceedings before the local courts the summons may be replaced by a form, filled in by the plaintiff and sent to the defendant by the court clerk.

3.15. Norway. Proceedings are initiated by means of a conciliation petition ("forliksklage") to the Conciliation Council. The petition has to name the parties as well as outline the nature of the dispute. The petition may be made orally or in writing.

After the Council has verified that the petition is in order, the Council will ensure that it is served on the defendant. Service will normally be by post. The defendant will be asked to give his version of the dispute, orally or in writing. If he does so, the parties will be required to appear for a Conciliation Council hearing.

Proceedings in the local courts are commenced by means of a writ ("stevning"). The writ has to name the court at which proceedings are to be commenced and the parties. The writ sets out the plaintiff's claim, the arguments supporting the claim, and the relief sought. The writ must be in writing and be signed by the plaintiff or his lawyer.

After the court has verified that the writ is in order, the court will ensure that it is served on the defendant. Service is primarily carried out personally at the domicile of the defendant, but may alternatively be by post. In some cases this will be followed by an initial court hearing, but normally the defendant is asked to serve a written defence ("tilsvar") to be submitted to the court by a specific date. Further written pleadings may be allowed before a court hearing is called.

3.16. Portugal. Process for a civil action begins with the filing of an initial petition (Petição Inicial). In that petition the plaintiff must:

(1) identify the parties and state the court where the action will be filed;
(2) indicate the nature of the proceedings, that is to say, whether they are common or special proceedings, and if they are common proceedings whether or not the proceedings are for summary process;

The Forms of Originating Process for Civil Litigation 43

(3) state the factual and legal background to the action and the relief sought;
(4) identify the value of the claim;
(5) specify those facts which the plaintiff considers proven or in dispute; the plaintiff may identify the list of witnesses and request other means of evidence at this stage. This means that the plaintiff may disclose to the court any evidence he intends to rely on, for example, by requesting the admission of documents into the procedure, or requesting that an examination, survey or evaluation be made of certain property, being either moveable goods or real property. The plaintiff is allowed to request evidence from the other parties.

If the petition filed is valid, the judge will order its service upon the defendant and require a defence (Contestação) to be lodged within 20 days. If no defence is lodged, the defendant is deemed to admit the facts pleaded in the petition. Apart from lodging the defence the defendant may at the same time introduce a counterclaim (Reconvenção). The plaintiff has eight days to lodge a reply (Réplica).

A petition is invalid when the claim and the cause of action are not indicated or are not intelligible, when the claim contradicts the cause of action, or where substantially incompatible claims are formulated. The consequence of an invalid petition is that the judge must reject it and all subsequent process becomes null and void.

An action will also be struck out, *inter alia*, where the parties lack either judicial personality or capacity or if the action is brought outside the limitation period. When the petition is struck out, the plaintiff has five days from the date of the order of the court either to appeal or file a new petition.

3.17. Spain. Process is initiated by a formal writ of judicial demand (Demanda) in which the claimant requests the court's assistance in resolving the dispute with the defendant. Process is not possible without a claim to initiate it and to determine the object of process and the contents of the future judgment.

In Spanish law, the demand always takes the form of a writ and begins with a general request to the court. The writ must contain details which identify the defendant (name, address, personal particulars, etc). The demand states succinctly the facts and grounds of law, and identifies, clearly and precisely, what the claimant is requesting.

The demand must be accompanied by a power of attorney proving that the claimant's representative (Procurador) can act as such. Any documentation showing the status of the claimant in the process must also be provided, (if the claimant, in turn, is the legal representative of any person or corporation), along with all documentation supporting the claimant's request.

3.18. Sweden. Civil proceedings are initiated through an application for summons ("stämningsansökan") to the District Court. The application must contain a specified claim, a detailed account of the facts, a statement of evidence and a note of the facts which establish the jurisdiction of the court. The application must be made in writing and signed by the plaintiff or his counsel.

When the court is satisfied as to the formal sufficiency of the application, the judge directs the issue of a summons and its service upon the defendant together with a copy of the plaintiff's application and any attached exhibits.

Service will initially be attempted by post. However, if there is no acknowledgment of receipt, the court will attempt personal service upon the defendant. If this fails, substituted service will be carried out. Upon request, a plaintiff may be granted the right to effect service on behalf of the court.

Following the issue of the summons by the court, the defendant is given an opportunity to state his defence by means of an answer ("svaromål") either in writing or at a preliminary court hearing. Normally, the defendant lodges a written answer whereupon one or more additional written pleadings are sent by the parties to the court and communicated to the other party before a preliminary court hearing is held.

Finally, it should be noted that a creditor may apply directly to a bailiff ("Kronofogdemyndigheten") to enforce a debt which is due. If the debtor makes no objections to the claim, the bailiff will issue an enforcement order in accordance with the creditor's application. If the debtor objects to the claim, the case will at the request of the creditor be referred to the competent district court.

3.19. Switzerland.

3.19:1. Ordinary Proceedings. Most civil actions are normally dealt with in ordinary proceedings. This includes actions for specific performance (Leistungsklagen) which encompass all claims for money irrespective of their underlying cause of action (contract, tort, unjust enrichment, etc), claims for any other form of performance, claims for prohibitory injunctions (Unterlassungsklagen) as well as actions for a change in a legal relationship (Gestaltungsklagen), or actions for a declaratory judgment (Feststellungsklagen).

In the Canton of Zurich, ordinary proceedings are generally begun by a petition to the Judge of the Peace (Friedensrichter) sitting at the court with jurisdiction (there are exceptions where this step is not necessary). The petition has to identify the parties and should give a short statement of the claim and the relief sought. It can be filed orally or by a written statement. Upon receipt of the petition, the Judge of the Peace serves both parties with a summons to appear before him. The defendant is served with a copy of the claimant's petition as well. The summons is usually served by post to the party personally or to an adult family member living in the same household or other legal representative, against signed acknowledgment of receipt. Other means of service (by bailiff, police, or publication) may be used if service by post cannot be effected.

At the hearing, the Judge of the Peace tries to negotiate a settlement between the parties. If he does not succeed, which is about 50 per cent of the time, he issues the claimant with the authorisation ("Weisung") to bring the action before the competent court.

If the whereabouts of the defendant are unknown or the defendant lives abroad and has no representative in Switzerland, the Judge of the Peace issues the claimant with authorisation to bring the claim before the competent court without summoning the parties to appear before him.

An oral hearing may also be waived by a party who has no domicile within the district of the court. The party may instead file a written statement. The other party then has the right to do the same.

The authorisation (Weisung) from the Judge of the Peace must be filed with the competent court within three months of issue. The litigation is deemed to have been commenced as from the date of the filing of the authorisation. If the action is to be dealt with by written proceedings, the authorisation must be accompanied by a written statement of claim containing all the factual allegations of the plaintiff, the evidence in support of such allegations (documents have to be attached, witnesses named), and the relief sought. If the statement of claim does not meet these requirements, but the authorisation has been properly filed, the court will grant the claimant a short extension of time to amend the statement of claim.

Upon receipt of the authorisation together with the statement of claim (or only the latter in proceedings where no authorisation is needed) the court decides *ex officio* on its venue and jurisdiction. If it considers that it has jurisdiction, and the proceedings are to be oral, the court serves both parties with a summons or, if the proceedings are to be in writing, the defendant is served with a copy of the statement of claim and a time-limit for the filing of a defence.

Service is effected by post (or other means if service by post is not possible) to the defendant personally or to his legal representative against a signed acknowledgment of receipt. If the defendant has his domicile abroad, service has to be effected through diplomatic channels unless special treaties provide for easier ways of service. Switzerland has signed and recently ratified the 1965 Hague Convention on the service of judicial and extrajudicial documents in civil or commercial matters.

Upon receipt of the service of originating process the defendant must enter an appearance. If the court has properly established its jurisdiction over the dispute, including the correct service of the originating process, then any silence on the part of the defendant will lead to the assumption by the court that the allegations of the claimant in his statement of claim are admitted by the defendant. The court will then base its judgment solely on the facts as they have been presented by the claimant.

The defendant may, in the first instance, limit his reply to challenging the jurisdiction of the court. The court will then have to decide the issue of jurisdiction before the proceedings can be continued (the claimant will be given the opportunity to file a brief as to the question of jurisdiction).

3.19:2. Summary Proceedings. Summary proceedings are initiated by an oral or written petition to the single judge. The petition must contain names and addresses of the parties, a short statement of the facts and the relief sought. The proceedings before the Judge of the Peace do not take place. Upon receipt of the petition the parties are served with a summons for a hearing. The defendant is further served with a copy of the petition (in the event that a written petition has been filed). Service is effected in the same way as in ordinary proceedings.

CHAPTER 4

CONDUCT OF THE PROCEEDINGS AND PRE TRIAL PREPARATION

4.01. The scope for gathering evidence from the opposing party and third parties. The essential components of legal proceedings which are identifiable in one form or another in all the systems operating in Europe are:

(1) allegations on matters of fact;
(2) the evidence which supports or contradicts those allegations; and
(3) argument on the law.

The variations between the different systems lie in the balance between the oral and written presentation of these elements and the extent to which the evidence and legal argument (as opposed to assertion) is rolled up into the exchange of pleadings and written submissions (which tend to form the introductory phases in all systems) or is left to the final phase of the hearing before the court.

Here, the contrast between the common law and civil law approaches is evident. In the common law system the judge passively reviews that which the adversaries place before him and lacks the scope of most civil law judges to take an inquisitorial role and seek out or require the parties to seek out what he considers relevant to the issues. To compensate for this the common law system places obligations on the adversaries themselves to disclose to one another all relevant documentary evidence so that the opponent may bring all such matters to the attention of the court. The procedure to enforce this process of "Discovery" therefore tends to be more extensive in the United Kingdom and Ireland than is typically the case in the continental system.

Furthermore the final hearing or trial in the common law system was developed to accommodate a jury consisting of a panel of 12 members of the general public unversed in legal matters. Whilst the jury has now all but disappeared from civil procedures, the trial process remains substantially unchanged concentrating on a single almost theatrical occasion focused on oral submissions and testimony for which all the issues must have been identified and all the evidence marshalled.

In contrast, civil law procedures involve a greater emphasis on written submissions extending both to legal argument and documentary evidence. The need for all the issues to be marshalled for one climactic hearing may be less evident. The court itself, rather than the advocates, may take the lead in interviewing witnesses and directing what matters it needs brought before it as the procedure progresses.

In this section we review the procedures for evidence gathering, including discovery, and the stages of procedure between inception and trial.

4.02. England and Wales. Once proceedings have commenced, the next stage is the exchange of pleadings. If no statement of claim, or particulars of claim in the County Court, have been served upon the defendant with the originating process, this must be served by the plaintiff. The defendant then submits his Defence and, if appropriate, Counterclaim. The plaintiff may serve a Reply to the Defence, but in the absence of a Reply he will be deemed to join issue with the Defence. If a Counterclaim is pleaded, the plaintiff must serve a Defence. In the pleadings the parties must set out fully the legal and factual basis for their claim and the nature of any relief sought. Pleadings may subsequently be amended, but at the hearing the evidence and argument led by the parties will be confined to their pleaded case. It is a rule of pleading that parties must not plead evidence. There are time limits for the service of the pleadings, but these are often subject to extension either by agreement between the parties or by application to the court.

Once pleadings have closed, the proceedings move to the stage of discovery. This is a comprehensive process and requires the parties to an action to disclose the existence of all documents (irrespective of whether or not they are favourable to the disclosing party's case) relevant to the case that are or were in their custody, possession or control. This includes disclosure of the existence of documents in which a party claims, *inter alia*, legal professional privilege.

After disclosure by list has taken place, the parties are entitled to inspect those documents on another party's list which are in that other party's custody, possession or control and which are not protected by privilege.

Conduct of the Proceedings and Pre Trial Preparation

Upon application by another party, the court has power to compel disclosure by a party. Failure to comply with the court order will be contempt of court and subject to the remedies available for contempt. Alternatively the court may strike out the offending party's pleadings and give judgment in favour of the other party. In practice the usual course is for the party seeking disclosure to ask in the first instance for an order that a party give discovery by a certain date. If that order is not complied with, the requesting party will ask the court to strike the other party out. At this stage the court will usually order discovery to be given within a stated period of time in the absence of which that party will be struck out and judgment given to the other side.

Actions are rarely struck out on the above grounds. If a party is struck out he may still apply to the court to set aside the striking-out order. The applicant must however show very good reason for the non-compliance with the court orders and may be penalised in costs.

In addition to discovery, a party may serve "interrogatories" on the other party relating to any matter in question between the applicant and the other party in the cause or matter which are necessary for disposing fairly of the cause or matter or for saving costs. It is for the party served with the interrogatories to apply to the court for an order that he does not have to answer them.

Apart from discovery between the parties, the courts have various powers to require disclosure from third parties. These powers include the power to grant a so-called Norwich Pharmacal Order. Such an order will be granted where, through no fault of their own, persons have got mixed-up in the tortious acts of others and have facilitated those acts. In this event the court may consider that the persons, while incurring no personal liability, are under a duty to assist the person who has been wronged by disclosing the identity of the persons involved and giving full information. Application for such an order is by way of writ issued against the third party indorsed with a claim for discovery. Interlocutory application seeking disclosure of the wrongdoer's identity can then be made to the Master on affidavit evidence.

Under section 7 of the Bankers Book's Evidence Act 1879 the court has the power to order a bank to allow the inspection of its books and copies to be made of the entries. If the order is to be made in relation to the account of a person not a party to the action, it should not ordinarily be made without notice to that person. Again, the application for inspection is made on application to the Master and supported by an affidavit.

Apart from its powers in respect of the production of evidence, the court has extensive interlocutory powers over the subject-matter of the proceedings. Orders specific to the preservation, detention or delivery-up of assets are dealt with in the following Chapter.

The court has a general discretion to grant interlocutory injunctive relief, whether or not such relief forms part of the relief to be sought at trial. The principal purpose of such relief is to preserve the situation pending the determination of the rights of the parties at trial. Generally injunctions will be in the negative, that is to say restraining certain actions. However, it is possible for a mandatory injunction to be granted if appropriate. Applications for injunctive relief are begun by summons, unless they are sufficiently urgent to justify *ex parte* application. Where interlocutory injunctive relief is sought before the substantive action has been issued, an injunction may be granted but on terms that the writ or originating summons be issued forthwith. In the High Court, application in the Queen's Bench Division is made to the Judge in Chambers. In the Chancery Division the application is made on motion. Any party seeking injunctive relief has to give a cross-undertaking to compensate the other party in damages should the relief sought subsequently be proved to have been unjustified.

Aside from interlocutory injunctive relief, a plaintiff may also feel that he has a sufficiently strong case that there can be no defence to his claim. In this instance it is open to him to apply for summary judgment. In the Queen's Bench Division such an application is made after the Statement of Claim has been served and after the defendant has given notice of intention to defend. The application is made in the first instance to the Master on affidavit evidence. In his affidavit the plaintiff must swear to his belief that there is no defence to the action. In reply the defendant must show that there is a triable issue. Where a plaintiff seeks summary judgment, knowing of the existence of a triable issue, he may be penalised in costs. Application for summary judgment is perhaps most appropriate in actions for liquidated debts and for payment of dishonoured bills of exchange or cheques.

If the court feels that the defendant has shown a triable issue such as to justify the grant of leave to defend but is concerned that the matter is either on the borderline or that the defence is a sham, the court may make the grant of leave conditional on payment into court of the sum in dispute or part thereof.

Conduct of the Proceedings and Pre Trial Preparation 51

An application for summary judgment may combined in the alternative with an application for an interim payment of any damages, debt or other sum. Similar procedures exist in the County Court.

A "Payment into Court" may be made voluntarily by a defendant and not solely pursuant to an order of the court. The possibility of paying money into court is particularly useful when a defendant wishes to settle an action on a "without prejudice" basis but also wishes to preserve his position as to any costs incurred after the offer of settlement has been made. "Without prejudice" negotiations are not revealed to the court at trial, so it is possible for a defendant to have a settlement offer refused prior to trial which is more than or equal to the amount subsequently recovered at trial and still be liable for the plaintiff's costs of the action. Paying money into court can prevent this happening. Prior to trial the defendant may pay into court the amount he considers the plaintiff will be awarded at trial plus a sum for the interest accrued on the capital sum up to the date of the payment-in. The payment into court will not be revealed to the judge at trial, but may be revealed to the court when the issue of the costs of the action is argued.

Once the defendant has paid money into court, the plaintiff is entitled to accept that money in settlement of his claim. If the plaintiff does so, he will also recover his costs up to the time of acceptance. Once the money paid into court has been accepted, all further proceedings in the action are stayed.

If the plaintiff does not accept the money paid into court and the amount recovered by the plaintiff at trial is less than or equal to the amount paid into court, the plaintiff will be required to pay the defendant's costs of the action from the date of the payment in. However, if the sum awarded at trial is greater than the amount paid in, the plaintiff will recover his costs in the usual way.

If the matter comes to trial, the strong oral tradition of the English system requires all evidence to be relied on by the parties to be proved at trial. Evidence is primarily given orally by the parties and witnesses on their behalf. Written depositions from witnesses may be admitted at trial but only with the agreement of the other parties or if they comply with the conditions of the Civil Evidence Act 1968 allowing certain categories of hearsay evidence to be admitted at trial when, in given circumstances, the witness cannot be brought to trial. Otherwise if documentary evidence is to be relied upon at trial, then a witness should be called to prove from his own knowledge the validity of such document. In practice this is often avoided by the parties agreeing the validity of the documents.

Although the English legal system remains committed to the oral tradition, witness statements are now generally taken by each side from their witnesses and exchanged with the other side, so that the issues between the parties are defined. The witness statement then generally stands as evidence-in-chief of the witness concerned. The maker of the statement will affirm his statement at trial and then be cross-examined by the other parties.

A party may wish to call expert evidence in support of his case. To do this, leave of the court is required and the parties must disclose the contents of any expert report to be relied on by them to the other parties before the hearing. In complicated cases there may also be a meeting of the experts prior to the trial in order to try and narrow the issues between them.

Legal argument between the parties takes place at trial. The general rule is that the plaintiff's counsel has the right to open the proceedings outlining the nature of his case. The plaintiff and his witnesses will then be heard followed by the defendant and his witnesses. Following the close of evidence, the defendant's counsel will make his closing speech with the plaintiff's counsel having a right of reply.

4.03. Scotland. Once the defender has received the writ he must submit his written defence. In the Court of Session the written defence (and any counterclaim) and the original Summons are then printed in a document called the Open Record. This document is then passed between the solicitors for all the parties and each side marks on it their adjustments to the claim or defence with each meeting the allegations of the other with denials, admissions, explanations or amplifications. Thereafter, normally after a period of eight weeks, the written pleadings are closed (the Closed Record) although in practice, the pleadings are almost invariably amended. The theory behind this process is (1) to narrow the areas in dispute as far as possible, and (2) to ensure that all the parties have fair notice of the other side's case since it is not permitted to lead evidence at the Proof of matters notice of which has not been given in the Closed Record. There is a substantially similar procedure in the Sheriff Court.

One interesting feature of the Scottish system is the opportunity to any party to argue purely legal issues arising in a case before the expense of a Proof of evidence occurs. Apart from arguing technical matters, such as that the written pleadings do not give adequate notice of the case, there are many cases in which the substantive legal arguments on the legal validity of a claim of defence take place in a legal debate before a single judge and result in a final resolution of the matter. Decisions at a legal debate are subject to appeal to the Inner House and then to the House of Lords.

Scotland has an elaborate system for the pre-proof recovery of documents. In most cases the procedure is by way of a Specification for Recovery of Documents. This is a document prepared by a party's lawyers which seeks the court's authority to recover all the documents specified in the order. Parties to the litigation can oppose the Specification or seek to have the ambit of the Recovery restricted. However, frequently, documents are sought from parties who are not parties to the case. If the judge grants the request, a non-party must comply with his order, but the documents can be lodged subject to a claim of confidentiality. These applications can be made at any stage in the litigation. The order, broadly speaking, can compel any holder of documents to come to the court to hand them over or to answer questions on oath as to where the documents are or to give reasons why certain papers should not be handed over. In practice, if agreement is not reached, a Commissioner (a lawyer appointed by the court) will be ordered to sift through the documents in order to ascertain which do legitimately fall within the ambit of the Specification.

Traditionally there was no requirement in Scotland to disclose the identity or existence of witnesses to the other party. This is still the position in the majority of cases in the Court of Session, except in certain actions for damages brought under the simplified optional procedure or cases which are specifically designated as commercial causes. In such exceptional cases, additional disclosure requirements are imposed on the parties by the Rules of Court. The parties must disclose the names and addresses of all their witnesses and prepare and exchange a list of all documents which are or have been in their possession relating to the matters at issue. Commercial causes are also subject to the fast track timetable with specialist judges and provide for the admittance of affidavit evidence. Broadly speaking, commercial causes relate to the construction of commercial documents or leases, banking disputes, sale or hire purchase of goods, carriage of goods and in summary any dispute of a business or commercial nature. The procedure is relatively new and the Court of Session is keen that the procedure should be utilised to ensure a speedier resolution of business and commercial disputes. Provision exists for remit to a specialist man of skill, for example where a special custom of trade is alleged.

A specialist procedure also exists for the resolution of certain Admiralty disputes, again with the emphasis on the need for speed.

The courts in Scotland have the power to grant interim orders either restraining actions (an interim interdict) or in certain limited areas ordering a positive action to be taken. These applications are made *ex parte* either by way of a separate action for interdict or in combination with an action involving other substantive matters. Detailed averments of the grounds for the application have to be made in the original petition or writ. There are no affidavits and the *ex parte* statements to the court are made on the authority of the counsel or solicitor. No formal undertakings in damages require to be given in the normal case. There exists in Scotland a procedure (the Caveat procedure) whereby a document can be lodged in court requiring a named solicitor to be contacted in the event of any interim order whether of an interim interdict, appointment of provisional liquidator or otherwise being applied for. This gives the defender the opportunity to be heard before an order is made. (This procedure does not cover search and seize orders — see Chapter 5).

Procedures exist in Scotland for the obtaining of summary decree (judgment), where the defence appears to be spurious, and also for the obtaining of interim decree where it is clear that some money is due but where the final amount cannot be ascertained until after Proof. With certain limited exceptions, evidence in Scotland is given orally although frequently parties will agree the contents of documents or reports to save the author having to speak to them. Expert evidence is frequently employed although there is no obligation in the majority of cases to disclose in advance the nature of that evidence.

At a Scottish Proof there are no opening speeches. The case commences with the evidence of the pursuer's witnesses followed by that of the defenders. The evidence is recorded in shorthand. Thereafter the pursuer's lawyer addresses the judge on the evidence as led and the legal consequences of that evidence and the defender has a right of reply.

4.04. Austria. There are special rules governing particular procedures, for example the rules governing the "Mahnklage" (see Chapter 3), but the majority of Austrian civil proceedings are carried out according to the oral tradition.

Conduct of the Proceedings and Pre Trial Preparation 55

After the writ has been served, the court will schedule the preliminary hearing, during which any initial objections to the proceedings can be made. It is at this hearing that a defendant should raise issues such as the lack of competence of the court to hear the matter or an application for security for costs. The court ascertains, in particular, if there is a defence to the claim. If not, the plaintiff applies for a default judgment (Versäumungsurteil). If the defendant decides to defend the action, he is allowed up to four weeks in order to put in his defence before the preliminary hearing. The court has the discretion to require a defendant to put in his defence immediately without having first arranged a preliminary hearing.

After service of the defence, the court will generally decide, taking into account the facts claimed by the parties, what evidence it will hear at the main hearing, identifying the issues it considers to be pertinent and on which it will hear evidence. In exceptional cases, the court requires further pleadings to be exchanged.

Admissible forms of evidence include documentary evidence, depositions from the parties, witness statements, expert testimony and where appropriate the inspection of property. Discovery is limited to the disclosure of the evidence which each party considers relevant to its own legal arguments.

There are no formal rules of evidence comparable to those in England and Wales; the court makes its decision after considering all the evidence presented to it.

If there is a danger that evidence may be lost, steps to preserve that evidence may be taken before the court where the hearing is being held or before the district court in whose district the objects to be inspected are situated or where the subject matter of an expert's testimony is to be found or where the persons to be questioned are situated.

Procedures for the preservation of testimony are principally to be heard *inter partes*; only if there is a danger of unacceptable delay can evidence be taken *ex parte*.

4.05. Belgium. Once the action has been begun, the parties must exchange their files of evidence and written submissions. There is no discovery process comparable with that of England and Wales. The parties simply have a duty to exchange those documents to be relied upon at hearing. However, if a party is believed to be suppressing evidence, the court may demand production of the document or a certified copy. The parties may also apply for interrogatories from the parties, but the decision to grant them is at the sole discretion of the judge.

Evidence may be adduced by the examination of witnesses where there is insufficient documentary evidence to prove relevant facts. However, witness evidence is only admissible at the discretion of the judge. Examination of the witnesses is the task of the judge and the parties may only put questions to a witness through the court.

4.06. Denmark. Details of the documentary and witness evidence to be relied upon must be appended to the writ.

Civil proceedings are governed by the negotiation principle. This means in practice that the judge plays a background role in the proceedings, leaving the presentation of evidence and argument to the discretion of the parties. This role is tempered by the principle of "material conduct of the proceedings" embodied in Article 339 of the Law on Civil Procedure, which places the court under a limited obligation to guide the parties and clarify the issues at stake.

Witness evidence is given orally, first in-chief and then by way of cross-examination. The court also has a power to examine the witness.

Pursuant to Chapter 19 of the Law on Civil Procedure each party may request the use of expert evidence. If the court is amenable to the proposition, it will appoint an expert witness to comment on the evidence. The court's evidence is put to the court both orally and in writing.

4.07. Finland. At the first stage, the parties exchange written submissions. In the absence of a reply from the defendant judgment in default may be given. If the matter cannot be decided on the basis of written documents, the preparation is continued in an adversarial oral session chaired by a single judge who takes an active role. At this session, the judge may direct the parties towards an amicable settlement or may dispose of the matter if it is sufficiently straightforward. Alternatively, the judge may make a disclosure order against a third party and can settle the expert witnesses to appear at the main hearing for the parties. He may also call his own expert witnesses.

The following stage is the main hearing if it has not been possible to resolve the matter at the preparatory stage. The main hearing, where witness evidence (including expert evidence) is also given, is oral. Normally it is not possible to refer to any new circumstances or new evidence at this stage.

Conduct of the Proceedings and Pre Trial Preparation 57

4.08. France. Commercial litigation is theoretically oral. No written documents are required to be submitted by the parties, except the originating summons, and any evidence they intend to lead. Overall there is a general freedom as to evidence and its form. Most commonly, evidence will consist of written documentation and affidavits. Oral witness evidence is extremely rare.

There is no general process of disclosure; each party must only disclose those documents on which they intend to rely. The court does have a power to *subpoena* from one party those documents requested by the other party and deemed necessary for the conduct of the litigation.

If third parties are in possession of evidence necessary for the conduct of the litigation, they are under a general duty to co-operate with the courts in the performance of their function. The court is entitled to *subpoena* such documents.

Although the court must leave it to the parties to determine the issues to be proved and the evidence in support, the court does have a power to appoint experts to help with the analysis of evidence.

4.09. Germany. Once the writ has been filed, the court decides whether there should be oral or written preliminary proceedings in preparation for the main oral hearing.

In preliminary written proceedings the scope of the action will be defined through the exchange of written briefs.

If the preliminary proceedings are oral, there will be an initial hearing after the filing of the defence. At this hearing the court will discuss with the parties the case and the state of the evidence in order to ensure that the matter can be dealt with properly at the main oral hearing.

Evidence is taken at the main oral hearings. At the conclusion of the last evidential hearing the judge may be able to make his decision or he may allow the parties an opportunity to make further written submissions. There will then be a final hearing to give the parties a last opportunity to address the court. In practice, this opportunity is used infrequently. Judgment will then either be declared at the end of that hearing or reserved for a later date.

The scope and substance of the evidence gathered is a matter primarily within the control of the parties and is carried out by motion (Beweisantritt) on the part of the party bearing the burden of proof. However, the process of evidence gathering is conducted by the court. Five forms of evidence are recognised:

inspection (Augenschein), witnesses (Zeugen), experts (Sachverständige), documents (Urkunden), and examination of the parties (Parteivernehmung).

The taking of evidence from witnesses is led by the court. After a witness has had an opportunity to give his evidence, he may be questioned, firstly by the court and then, with the permission of the court, by the legal representatives for the various parties.

Contrary to the practice in England and Wales, there is no general duty to disclose documents in Germany. There are exceptions to this general rule. The exceptions concern circumstances where a party has referred to documents himself and where a party is under a specific duty at law to disclose certain types of document. Behind this approach to discovery lies the principle that litigation should be decided on the basis of the presentation by the parties (Verhandlungsgrundsatz), even though this may or may not represent a full and true picture of the case.

The nature of the duty of disclosure alters in those proceedings where the court has a specific duty of investigation under civil law (Untersuchungsgrundsatz). However, save where the validity of a document is contested by the other party, this duty is limited to proceedings such as matrimonial proceedings, affiliation matters and guardianship proceedings.

In practice a photocopy of relevant documents will be delivered with the pleadings. Such delivery equates to documentary evidence. A consequence of delivery is that statements of fact evidenced by the documents are considered uncontested and further presentation of the original is unnecessary. Only in proceedings based on documentary evidence must the original or a certified copy thereof be attached to the pleadings.

The scope for interim preservation of evidence is limited, firstly as to the types of evidence affected and secondly as to circumstance. Applications are restricted to those for inspection or the interrogation of witnesses or experts. An application can not be used for the discovery of documents. Secondly, either the opposing party must consent to the application or there must be a significant risk of loss or increased difficulty in the use of the evidence before the beginning of civil proceedings. Relevant circumstances would include the dangerous illness of a witness, extended travel overseas, the deterioration of evidence which will have to be inspected, or the possibility that by taking the evidence at this stage, the entire proceedings can be avoided.

Application for an order preserving evidence is made to the court in which the main dispute is pending, or, in case of imminent danger, in the court for the district in which the person to be interrogated is present or the object to be preserved is located. In support of the application the applicant must provide details of the defendant, an allegation of the facts to be proved, the means of proof giving names and details of witnesses and experts to be examined, together with reasons justifying the application.

If the application is granted, the witness must be properly summoned to a hearing for the taking of the evidence. The evidence will be recorded by the court and the records maintained at that court.

4.10. Greece. Generally civil and commercial litigation follows a so-called "Ordinary Procedure" (Taktiki Diadikasia). However in order to provide a quicker form of litigation for certain types of action, Greek law has introduced various special procedures (Eidikai Diadikasiai). The types of dispute affected include:

(1) Issue of Payment Orders (Diatagi Pliromis);
(2) Disputes over Negotiable Instruments (Diaforai ek Pistotikon Titlon);
(3) Disputes between landlord and tenant and disputes between owners and managers of a condominium (Misthotikai Diaforai);
(4) Labour Disputes (Ergatikai Diaforai);
(5) Disputes over payment of fees for, inter alia, lawyers, notaries, doctors, dentists, and engineers.

A special voluntary jurisdiction exists for certain actions, in particular the ratification of a foreign judgment, or arbitration award. Unlike most other forms of civil procedures, which are adversarial, the voluntary jurisdiction is governed by an inquisitorial approach led by the judge.

The course of litigation is based upon a written pre-trial procedure. There is no process of discovery (save in limited exceptional cases requiring the parties to go through a cumbersome procedure). The parties develop their case on the basis of the evidence available to them. Subject to a duty to observe the rules of morality, good business ethics and good faith, there is no absolute obligation upon a party to disclose evidence harmful to his case.

To alleviate the workload of the multi-member Court of First Instance in certain cases the plaintiff may, when filing the action, request the judge fixing the hearing dates for the cases before the multi-member Court of First Instance, to order that the case be tried according to Article 238–GCCP under which the court is not obliged to issue an interim (interlocutory) judgment (although it may do so). In such a case, the parties must at the hearing, in addition to the documentary evidence produced with the pleadings (which must be filed at least three working days prior to the hearing), examine and cross-examine all their witnesses. In other words the procedure applied in such cases is the one applied for in cases brought before the single-member Court of First Instance.

This procedure is permitted only if the case is simple or evidenced by documents and has been introduced pursuant to Law 2207/1994.

Prior to the hearing of the case, the parties must submit their written submissions (Protaseis), accompanied by all the relevant documentary evidence in support. Failure to comply with this obligation means that the party is deemed not to have entered a proper appearance and will be considered procedurally absent.

A plaintiff's written submissions do not necessarily have to contain an analysis of the law upon which the action is founded as the court is assumed to know the law. However, in practice, such analysis is included in the submissions.

A defendant must not only address the merits of the claim in his submissions, but must also deal with any procedural objections, for example, the existence of an arbitration agreement. Failure to address these issues at first instance will prevent a defendant raising them subsequently.

A defendant may begin a counterclaim either by separate originating process served upon the plaintiff at least eight clear working days prior to the hearing of the action or by the written submissions to be submitted for the hearing. In the latter event, the submissions must be filed with the court at least eight clear working days prior to the hearing date.

Usually under the ordinary procedure, the hearing before the multi-member Courts of First Instance is completed by the filing of the written submissions and the appearance before the court of the litigant with his attorney or by the attorney alone at the date of hearing. Even before the single-member Courts of First Instance, the Courts of Peace, and the cases adjudicated under the voluntary jurisdiction, the procedure is in writing unless the litigants wish to examine witnesses. It should be noted here that the attorney appearing for his client is assumed to have the authorisation to do so, unless the opposing party disputes his authority. In the event of such a dispute, the court orders the attorney to produce his credentials (*i.e.* power of attorney).

In the ordinary procedure of the single-member Courts of First Instance, the parties are entitled to examine their witnesses *viva voce*. In the ordinary procedure of the multi-member courts, after completion of the hearing the court will either give a final or an interlocutory judgment. An interlocutory judgment may be given where the court considers it needs further evidence in order to form an opinion on the merits of the case or any point of law (if the applicable law is foreign).

In the special procedures, the trial is conducted by written submissions and oral argument; witness evidence is given orally at the hearing. After the hearing the court will reserve judgment until a subsequent date.

The forms of admissible evidence are:

(a) the confession (omologia);
(b) the autopsy (autopsia);
(c) expert opinion (pragmatognomosyni);
(d) witnesses (martyres);
(e) examination of the litigants;
(f) oath (orkos);
(g) documents (egrapha);
(h) judicial presumptions (tekmiria).

The commonest forms of evidence comprise documents and witnesses. Evidence from witnesses will be allowed where the plaintiff cannot obtain the documentary evidence for physical or moral reasons, or if the documents have been lost, or, if in the circumstances of the case, witness evidence is justified.

Witnesses will either be examined at the hearing of the case or by way of depositions before a judge or before a justice of the peace or consul following an interim or interlocutory judgment.

In support of the evidence gathering process, the court has power to grant orders for the preservation of evidence and to allow a plaintiff to enter and search premises and seize and preserve evidence found there.

4.11. Ireland. Once proceedings have been commenced, the role of pleadings will vary depending on the court before which the action is brought. No pleadings are usually exchanged in the district court. In the circuit court the only pleading required apart from the civil bill is a defence. Before the High Court the rules of procedure provide for an exchange of pleadings similar to those pertaining in England and Wales.

As in England and Wales the purpose of the pleadings is to define the issues between the parties. Pleadings do not normally contain legal submissions, but state the material facts on which each party will rely.

In common with the system in England and Wales, Ireland has a comprehensive procedure for the discovery of documentary evidence. Prior to trial the parties may or must, if ordered to do so by the court, disclose to each other by affidavit all material documents in their possession or power. Should a party fail to disclose a material document or refuse to disclose such a document, the other party can apply to the court for an order requiring discovery of the document. Following discovery, the parties are entitled to inspect the documents disclosed, unless they are privileged. If a document is referred to in the pleadings of a party, the other party can insist on its production by way of a notice to produce.

Privilege from production is granted to documents covered, *inter alia*, by legal professional privilege and includes correspondence between solicitor and client and "without prejudice" correspondence.

Apart from the process of discovery by document, a party may call for discovery by interrogatories, calling upon the other party to admit or deny facts. There is however little use made of witness depositions.

Pursuant to the Bankers' Books Evidence Acts 1879 to 1989 the High Court has the power to make orders for inspection of banking records, including microfilm and electronic media, relevant to the proceedings, whether or not the bank concerned is a party to the action. The court also has the power to allow a plaintiff to obtain disclosure of documents held by third parties.

If there has been any default in pleadings or in the giving of discovery by the defendant, the plaintiff may apply to the court for judgment. Conversely, if there has been default by the plaintiff in delivering his statement of claim or in giving discovery the defendant may apply to the court to have the plaintiff's claim struck out. Such orders are rarely granted but exert pressure on the party in default to provide the missing pleading or to give discovery.

When pleadings have closed and the case has been certified as being ready for trial the action may be set down for hearing (usually by the plaintiff). A plenary action will normally take between six and eighteen months to come to trial from the date proceedings were issued.

The true adversarial nature of the Irish courts places emphasis upon giving oral evidence on oath. A witness may be compelled to appear in court to give oral testimony or to produce a document. Written witness statements are only allowed exceptionally. However, the court does have the power to order trial

Conduct of the Proceedings and Pre Trial Preparation 63

by affidavit where appropriate. Such may be the case where the facts are not in dispute and the issues are largely ones of legal argument.

Argument before the court is invariably oral, although in certain types of appeal to the Supreme Court written submissions may be made in advance, summarising the arguments to be advanced at the appeal. In addition, by way of a Practice Direction, the High Court has encouraged written legal submissions in advance of a trial where substantial legal issues are likely to arise.

4.12. Italy. Proceedings before the first instance courts are divided into three phases:

(1) the introductory phase;
(2) the discovery phase;
(3) the decision-making phase.

The introductory phase covers the exchange of pleadings. The pleadings served by both the plaintiff and the defendant must include a statement of the evidence the party intends to lead and the documents to be disclosed.

The process of evidence gathering is continued within the discovery phase. The discovery phase is divided into three elements: treatment of case, examination of evidence and reference of the case to the judging panel. The discovery phase is begun by a hearing before the investigating judge attended by legal representatives. At that hearing the judge will consider what further orders are required in the light of the issues between the parties. This might include an adjournment for the parties to submit further written details of their case.

Following this hearing and gathering of any further evidence ordered, the judge will form his own independent view of the evidence. Italian law prescribes closely the forms of admissible evidence. Alongside those forms of evidence, the judge may also rely upon expert opinion and inspection of the books of either the parties or third parties. Neither expert opinion nor an examination of the books is strictly speaking treated as formal evidence.

Following the gathering of evidence under the control and at the instigation of the investigating judge, the case is referred to a panel of judges for final hearing (the decision-making phase). In actions before the Justice of Peace and the Magistrate the case is decided by the judge having investigated the case and is not referred to a panel of judges.

4.13. Luxembourg. There is an obligation on parties to any litigation to disclose any necessary documentary evidence upon which they wish to rely. There is, however, no general obligation of disclosure, save that the court has a power to order discovery of documents known to exist. Any witnesses the parties wish to rely on may either give their evidence orally or in writing. If the evidence is to be oral, a witness hearing will be scheduled. At the hearing only the judge has the right to question the witnesses but the parties may suggest questions to be asked.

4.14. The Netherlands. Proceedings in the Netherlands are primarily conducted in writing. Supporting documentation for allegations in pleadings are generally annexed thereto. There is no formal process for general discovery, but, if a particular document is in the possession of only one party, the court has the discretion to put the burden of proof for matters to which the document relates on that party. There is power to compel disclosure from another party of documents linked to a legal relationship to which he is party. If a party has lost written evidence of facts, that party is able to order disclosure by the other parties of documents proving those facts.

Where it is relevant to the dispute, the court has power to inspect the books of one or both parties. In the presentation of evidence the court will take an essentially passive role. However, the court may order the attendance of witnesses at court and direct the taking of oral evidence.

Although the court may accept witness testimony in writing, it prefers such evidence to be given orally. The hearing of such witnesses will be ordered as interlocutory proceedings, and may be on one or several occasions. At the hearing, the judge will dictate a summary of the evidence given, which will be typed and put to the witness for signature at the same hearing.

Matters of legal argument are generally submitted in writing. When the proceedings are before the Arrondissementsrechtbank or a higher court the parties are allowed an opportunity for oral argument.

4.15. Norway. As the procedure and pre-trial preparations in the Conciliation Councils are quite informal and of limited consequence, the following passage will deal with proceedings before the local court.

During the pre-trial preparations the parties will normally exchange a number of further written pleadings. This process mainly consists of the parties specifying the documentary and witness evidence to be relied upon in support of their claims and counterclaims. In order to get hold of such evidence a party will often apply to the court for an order that the other party disclose certain particular documents it is believed to have in its possession. If the application is sufficiently specific, the other party will then be under an obligation to produce the documents even if it is detrimental to its own claims.

The pre-trial preparations will be followed by a court hearing in which the parties present the arguments and evidence in support of their claims and counterclaims. The presentation must be oral, implying that any documentary evidence needs to be proved orally at the hearing (in summary or in full, at the parties' own discretion). As civil and commercial proceedings are governed by the negotiation principle, the presentations are to a large extent left to the discretion of the parties. However, the court is under a limited obligation to ensure that the issues at stake are sufficiently clarified. The judge may thus examine the parties and witnesses if it is felt to be necessary. Witness evidence and that of the parties themselves is given by oral examination, first in-chief and then by way of cross-examination.

Each party may request that one or more expert witnesses be appointed. If the court allows expert evidence, that evidence will also be given orally at the hearing.

4.16. Portugal. Following the close of pleadings, the examining judge may decide that the action is suitable for immediate judgment and set a date for a hearing (Audiência Preparatoria) at which he will seek to reconcile the parties. If this is not possible the judge will issue a decision (Despacho Saneador) stating that the action is to continue and selecting the relevant facts. Those facts considered proven will be noted in a specification (Especificação) and the ones still to be proved inserted in a questionnaire (Questionario). The judge's decision can be appealed. Thereafter the parties have ten days to file their list of witnesses and list any other evidence. Any documents to be put before the court should have been filed prior to the judge's decision. Documents can be submitted subsequently any time up to the first instance decision. However, there is a proviso that, unless a party can show that it was not possible to file the documents prior to the "Despacho Saneador", a fine is payable on those documents submitted late.

The court has the power, at the request of one of the parties, to require the other party to produce specific documents. If a party does not produce a document the court is entitled to take this fact into account for the purposes of reaching its decision. It is open to a party to challenge a declaration from the producing party that he does not have the document.

Third parties can be ordered by the court to disclose documents in their possession upon the request of an interested party. The interested party must however specify the facts he will rely on the document to prove.

Witness evidence will generally be given at trial. There are, however, limited possibilities for written depositions to be admitted in evidence. Oral argument may also take place at trial. There is then a supplementary regime, allowing written argument from the parties for a period of eight days after trial. The court has 15 days from trial within which to reach a decision.

4.17. Spain. Progression from one procedural step to another is regulated by the court, which deems each phase of the process as completed without the need for any action by the parties.

Before the claim is filed the plaintiff may attempt to settle the dispute with the defendant before the court of first instance. If both parties appear before the court but do not settle, the plaintiff is charged with the expenses. If the parties do settle, the court will enforce the agreement. Failure to settle does not prejudice the rights of either party to settle at any point thereafter.

Within the Spanish system there is provision for the disclosure of documents. Different regulatory regimes apply depending upon whether the documents are public documents or private documents. Disclosure can be obtained from third parties holding relevant documents.

Where banks are the parties to proceedings, they are subject to the ordinary principles of disclosure. If banks are approached as third parties to provide documents which are their property, they can be required to reveal those documents provided the judge considers the documents essential to judgment.

Oral witness testimony is taken by the investigating judge, who will then present the evidence to the court in a written form and read it to the court.

There are limited measures for the preservation of evidence and the prevention of the disappearance of witnesses or documents.

Information regarding the circumstances concerning the future defendant or other matters which it is necessary to know in order to file the demand may be obtained through a process of

Conduct of the Proceedings and Pre Trial Preparation 67

Preliminary Measures (Diligencias Preliminares). In this way the subsequent process is made easier, although issue of proceedings does not take place in the strict sense. Preliminary Measures follow a separate procedure and their use is limited to five situations:

(1) to request a sworn statement from the person against whom the demand will be filed setting out facts about him, which are necessary for the claim;
(2) to request inspection of any moveable object involved in the dispute;
(3) to request discovery of a will by a person purporting to be heir or legatee;
(4) to request discovery of title deeds or documents concerning an object that has been sold and which is the subject of the law suit;
(5) to request presentation of documents and accounts from a company or association by a partner or co-owner in possession thereof.

Jurisdiction for Preliminary Measures rests with the court with authority to handle the subsequent process. The parties to the Preliminary Measures are those who will appear as claimant and defendant to the substantive proceedings.

In the course of proceedings for Preliminary Measures, it is possible to apply for Precautionary Measures (Medidas Cautelares), such as a deposit. However Preliminary Measures should not be confused with such precautionary steps.

Although not strictly a Preliminary Measure, it is possible to request witness evidence to be taken early in circumstances when, due to the age of a witness or to any other risk to a witness's health or when the witness is due to depart to a place rendering communication difficult, the rights of the claimant could be prejudiced if the evidence is not taken early.

4.18. Sweden. The pre-trial preparations, following the summons application, normally consist of additional written pleadings from both parties. At this stage, each party will respond to its opponent's arguments on facts and law and will specify the oral and written evidence upon which it will rely to support its claim or defence.

In order to secure the provision of relevant documents which are in the possession of the other party, the court can be requested to issue an order for the production of such documents.

68   Conduct of the Proceedings and Pre Trial Preparation

Following the written preparation, a preliminary court hearing will usually be held. At this hearing, the parties present their claims and counterclaims and the arguments and evidence in support. The court will allow written pleadings or affidavits to be read aloud only if it decides that it will facilitate the understanding of a submission or for any other reason will be of advantage to the handling of the case. The judge in charge of the case will summarise the facts and identify the main points of dispute.

Civil and commercial proceedings take an adversarial form so that the judge leaves it to the parties to argue the case and present their evidence. The court, however, is obliged to ensure that the disputed issues are sufficiently clarified and, accordingly, the judge may ask questions of the parties and witnesses if he considers it necessary.

Oral evidence is provided by way of examination in court by the party calling the witness and then by way of cross-examination by the opposing party.

Each party may request that one or more expert witnesses ("sakkunnig") are appointed. The expert witness may give his statement in writing but will normally also be heard in person if requested by a party. In addition, the court may direct that the expert witness be heard in person.

4.19. **Switzerland.** In Switzerland proceedings are divided into three main phases:

(1) *the introductory phase*, where the parties make their allegations of the facts, state the evidence they wish to present to the court in order to support the alleged facts, state the relief sought, and present their legal argument on the case;

(2) *the discovery phase*, where witnesses and experts are heard, documents are presented, and any inspections held by the court;

(3) *the decision-making phase*, where the court discusses the case and decides on it by rendering a first instance judgment.

Finally, after the first instance judgment has been given, the judgment may be revised on appeal.

4.19:1. **Introductory Phase.** The introductory phase is either oral or written. In ordinary proceedings it is usually written. As a general principle, the parties have to present all

Conduct of the Proceedings and Pre Trial Preparation 69

their factual allegations together with supporting evidence in their first written pleadings, i.e. in the statement of claim and in the defence. In complicated cases the court may order a second exchange of written pleadings before or after the first court hearing.

At a certain stage of the proceedings, which may vary slightly from canton to canton, as well as for different types of proceedings, but at the latest at the end of the introductory phase, the parties have to have presented all their factual allegations. Thereafter, the introduction of new allegations is only possible under specific limited circumstances, for example, if the party was prevented from presenting the allegation in time through no fault of its own or if the alleged fact can be established by the court of its own motion or can be immediately proved by documents.

4.19:2. Discovery Phase. After the termination of the first phase the court decides on the factual allegations it deems relevant for its decision on the case and on which it will, therefore, allow evidence to be presented by the parties.

However, the court is usually bound by the facts that have been introduced by the parties and has no right to make further investigations in order to find "the truth". Only in a few cantons, do the procedural laws provide for the court to be able to request further evidence from the parties, and only in exceptional cases. Therefore, if the parties agree on certain facts (which is deemed to be the case if the defendant fails to contest a fact alleged by the claimant), the court must accept those facts as the basis for their decision.

Evidence is only to be presented in support of or against allegations on which the parties disagree, and which are considered relevant by the court for its decision. The question of relevance is a question of law and as such may be subject to revision in appellate proceedings.

The principles set out above do not apply in certain types of cases where the court has a legal obligation to investigate the facts ("Untersuchungsgrundsatz"). Such cases include affiliation proceedings, actions by children against their parents for financial support, or labour disputes.

The discovery phase is usually initiated by an ordinance of the court where all the alleged and contested facts which need to be proved are set out together with the identity of the party who bears the burden of proof for each alleged fact (and who will have to bear the legal consequences if the court is not persuaded by the evidence presented). The other party always has the right to present contrary evidence.

The forms of evidence which may be used by the parties are listed in the cantonal procedural laws. In the Canton of Zurich the following forms of evidence are recognised:

(1) depositions of the parties (under disciplinary sanctions ("persönliche Befragung") or — under certain conditions — second depositions under stronger criminal sanctions ("Beweisaussage"));
(2) depositions of third parties as witnesses ("Zeugen");
(3) documentary evidence ("Urkunden");
(4) expert opinion ("Gutachten") and local inspection ("Augenschein") by the court.

Witnesses are questioned by the court. At the end of the deposition counsel for the parties have the opportunity to ask the witness additional questions, usually through the court. Certain close relatives of a party can refuse to testify. Furthermore, every witness can refuse to testify on matters that might be to his detriment or to the detriment of such close relatives. Government officials, attorneys, priests, physicians, and their employees, as well as other professionals who are under a duty of silence or who are working on the basis of a relationship of confidence, may invoke special privileges. Otherwise, witnesses are under a duty to testify which can be enforced by way of sanctions (fines and (theoretically) imprisonment up to 10 days).

Parties to a suit must disclose documents that are in their possession. If a party refuses disclosure, the court may draw inferences adverse to that party. Third parties and government agencies must disclose documents that are in their possession and which are relevant to the proceedings. The limits to this discovery obligation are similar to those mentioned above in connection with witness depositions which are applied by analogy.

The taking of evidence is administered by the court. The court takes the depositions of the parties and witnesses; it orders the disclosure of documents, assigns the experts and drafts the questions to be submitted to them, and performs the inspections.

At the end of the discovery phase the parties are given the opportunity to comment on the results of the discovery.

Pre-trial discovery does not exist in Switzerland. Only in exceptional cases where it might be impossible for a party

Conduct of the Proceedings and Pre Trial Preparation 71

to gather the evidence at a later stage can the necessary discovery be obtained by summary proceedings before the local single judge. Appropriate cases would include applications for the deposition of an old or seriously ill witness who might pass away by the time court proceedings take place, or for the inspection of a perishable object under litigation, for the production of documents where the claimant can show strong prima facie evidence that at a later stage the production of the documents would be impossible or at least more difficult, etc. Where necessary, the summary proceedings may take place even before the main procedings have been initiated.

Actions which are pursued by summary proceedings are characterised by a limited discovery phase. Only limited means of evidence may be used (documents, inspection, depositions of the parties) and prima facie evidence is sufficient.

4.19:3. Decision-making Phase. Finally, in the decision-making phase the court assesses the results of the discovery phase. Such assessment takes place at the court's discretion (nach freiem Ermessen), but the exercise of that discretion cannot be arbitrary. The court decides the claim on the basis of the facts it deems to have been established.

CHAPTER 5

INTERIM PROTECTION OF ASSETS PENDING TRIAL

5.01. Introduction. Litigation is increasingly deployed as a tool to attain commercial objectives, not through the judgment of the court but by using the procedure as a means of pressure to force a commercial settlement. In this context, a great deal of the work of litigation lawyers is occupied not with the final trial but with applications for temporary measures (interlocutory orders) for assets to be frozen or protected pending trial. In practice, this serves as often as not as the lever for negotiated settlement.

The Brussels Convention provided for the first time a common system for temporary orders made in one contracting state to be enforced by registration in another. This system has been maintained and adopted in the Lugano Convention.

The United Kingdom in particular has in recent years rapidly developed the powers of courts to freeze assets by forbidding a defendant subject to their jurisdiction, from dealing with them both domestically and abroad. The Conventions now permit the executive powers of courts in other jurisdictions to be used to enforce such measures directly where the assets are actually located.

The system of registration is discussed separately in Chapter 10. Here we touch on the types of measure available on an interlocutory basis in the various domestic systems.

5.02. England and Wales. The courts have wide-ranging interlocutory powers, exercisable in various forms, to protect assets pending trial. The powers may be used both against assets which may be the subject matter of the dispute between the parties and in respect of a party's assets generally in order to ensure that he is able to meet any judgment debt accruing. Where sufficient urgency can be shown, or there is a risk that the party in question when informed of the interlocutory proceedings will dispose of the assets in question before the hearing takes place, the initial application can be made *ex parte* for an order pending an *inter partes* hearing. As with all forms of interlocutory injunctive relief, the party seeking the order will have to give a cross-undertaking to compensate the other party for any damage done by an order which is subsequently found to be unjustified.

On the application of any party to the proceedings the court may make an order for the detention, custody, preservation, or delivery up of any property which is the subject-matter of the proceedings. Additionally, the court may order the inspection of any such property in the possession of a party to the cause or matter. Application for such orders is generally made by summons issued by the plaintiff after the commencement of proceedings or by the defendant after giving notice of intention to defend.

A specific form of order for the detention or preservation of the subject-matter of a claim or the documents relating thereto is the Anton Piller Order. Named after the plaintiff in the case where the order first came to prominence, such an order empowers the plaintiff to enter the defendant's premises and search for material documents and articles. Application for the order is most often used in intellectual property actions. Where a plaintiff can show a good prima facie case that the potential or actual damage is very serious, that the defendant has in his possession incriminating materials, documentary or otherwise, and that there is a real risk that such material will be destroyed before any *inter partes* application is made, then an order may be granted *ex parte*. It is, however, subject to strict controls by the court to ensure that the order is not used oppressively.

Apart from orders concerning the actual subject matter of any action, the court may grant an interlocutory order restraining a defendant dissipating or otherwise disposing of his assets so as to make any judgment worthless or hard to enforce. Such an order is commonly known as the Mareva Injunction, again after the plaintiff in the case where the order first came to prominence. The usual practice is for the order to be made *ex parte* initially. For this reason the plaintiff bears an onerous burden of full and frank disclosure as to the true merits of his case and any other matters it is material for the court to know. Failure to meet this burden may lead to the injunction being discharged on application by the respondent and the applicant being liable for any damage suffered by the respondent as a result of the order.

Application can also be made for the appointment of a receiver. The court may grant such an application where it seems "just or convenient". The grant of an order appointing a receiver may be supported by any ancillary or incidental injunctive relief necessary.

5.03. Scotland. The Scottish courts have statutory power to order the inspection, production and recovery of documents and other property which might be used in subsequent court proceedings. These orders can be granted before service of proceedings and, if successful, result in an order allowing a court-appointed Commissioner to enter the defender's premises to search for and remove material documents and articles. Thereafter, the materials or documents seized are lodged in court and before the petitioner can be given access to them the respondent has the opportunity to object. The procedure is essentially one to be employed where there is a suspicion that incriminating material may be destroyed.

Scottish law permits certain special forms of procedure to protect the pursuer and freeze assets to which the defender might otherwise have access. Even prior to the service of proceedings, or at any time during the proceedings the pursuer can "arrest" assets in the hands of third parties but which that third party is due to pay, or account for, to the defender. The effect of such an arrestment is that the money or goods is frozen in the hands of the third party and in due course, once a decree is obtained, an order (a decree of furthcoming) can be obtained whereby that property is made over to the pursuer. The most simple example is a bank account. At any time in a Scottish action the defender's bank account can be frozen by simply serving an arrestment order on the bank. The obtaining of a warrant allowing arrestment is a formality.

5.04. Austria. The court can order a provisional injunction (Einstweilige Verfügung) prior to commencement of, or during, court proceedings and during enforcement proceedings in order to secure the rights of one of the parties.

Interim protection for pecuniary claims is possible when it is probable that without such relief the defendant would damage, destroy, conceal, sell or dispose of his assets, especially through agreements with third parties, and thereby prevent or considerably hinder the collection of monies. Interim protection will not, however, be granted if the plaintiff could already begin enforcement proceedings.

Provisional injunctions in respect of pecuniary claims may be put into effect by orders for the detention and administration of the defendant's movable assets. The various forms of order may include orders requiring the deposit of funds, prohibiting the sale or pledging of movable assets (such orders render sales or pledges contrary to the order invalid) and attaching injunctions against third parties against whom the defendant has a monetary claim or a claim for goods or services.

Provisional injunctions may also be issued to secure claims other than pecuniary ones if there is a perceived danger that the pursuit or realisation of the claim in question may be prevented or considerably hindered by changes made in the circumstances surrounding the claim. Matters likely to lead to the grant of an order include the possibility that otherwise any judgment would have to be enforced abroad or the possibility of a risk of violence or irrevocable damage to property.

Potential orders the court may make include orders for (1) the deposit at court of movables in the possession of the defendant which are the subject of the plaintiff's claim or, if the objects are not suitable for deposit at court, the appointment of a trustee; (2) the appointment of an administrator over movables or immovables or intangible rights claimed by the plaintiff; (3) for the transfer of the property into the custody of the plaintiff; (4) an order to the defendant obliging him to take such steps as may be deemed necessary to preserve the property concerned or the status quo; (5) the prohibition of the defendant from acting to the detriment of the property; (6) an injunction on the sale, mortgage or pledging of property or rights which have been registered publicly and which are claimed by the plaintiff; and (7) an injunction against third parties in cases where the defendant has a claim against the third party for payment or for the delivery up of objects claimed by the plaintiff.

Provisional injunctions are rarely imposed in cases regarding pecuniary claims. They are, however, regularly imposed in disputes involving intangible property.

Provisional injunctions are granted for a limited period of time, generally until such time as the judgment becomes final. If a provisional injunction is imposed prior to commencement of the proceedings, the plaintiff has a limited period of time within which he must bring an action. Should no action be brought before the deadline, the injunction becomes invalid. Both the plaintiff and the defendant can be ordered to make a payment into court as a form of security, so as to prevent potential losses or delays in the imposition of a provisional injunction.

5.05. Belgium. The commonest forms of provisional measure for the protection of assets are the saisie-Arrêt (attachment on money owed to the defendant by a third party) and saisie conservatoire (attachment on moveables or immoveables). Such orders are enforced by the bailiffs on the basis of a proof of title (for example: executory judgment, notarial deed, invoices, letters of exchange, cheques (a court order is required in respect of immoveable property)). Otherwise the court may make an order for such measures on an *ex parte* application.

Orders for the delivery-up and preservation of evidence are easily obtained upon *ex parte* application.

Orders for the inspection of bankers' books are not generally available in civil or commercial cases.

Orders for the appointment of receivers ("sequestres") to enter and protect assets or documents may be easily obtained either on an *ex parte* application or an application by summons.

There is no system for payments into court.

5.06. **Denmark.** Danish law provides for two forms of provisional measure; namely an attachment of assets and a prohibitive injunction. Application for such measures are made to the sheriff's court. Before a plaintiff can seek either an attachment of the defendant's assets, or an injunction in damages, he must provide a cross-undertaking in damages. Once an order for attachment or an injunction has been made, the plaintiff must apply for an order confirming the attachment or injunction either as part of the main proceedings commenced within seven days or, if the main proceedings are already under way, by a separate application within seven days. Even if the defendant offers security for the plaintiff's claim thus staying the attachment or injunction, the plaintiff must still apply for the confirmatory order.

Attachment will prevent the defendant from disposing of assets contrary to the plaintiff's claim. An injunction will be used to prevent the defendant from acting contrary to the plaintiff's interest. The plaintiff must establish that the defendant's proposed actions are contrary to his rights and that the defendant will otherwise carry out those acts. The plaintiff must also show that he will not be adequately protected by relying on his means of legal redress against the defendant. The court will refuse an injunction where the harm caused by granting it will outweigh the harm otherwise to be suffered by the plaintiff.

Denmark does not have any form of order equivalent to the Anton Piller Order.

At the request of a party the court may order a third party to disclose documents relevant to the case, save where those documents fall within certain exempted categories. The requesting party must however establish the facts to which it is alleged the disclosure of the documents is relevant. In deciding whether to make the order, the court will balance the interests of the third party and the other party to the case in keeping the contents of the documents secret against the interest of the plaintiff in disclosure of the document.

Any person may demand sight of documents which have been submitted to or prepared by an administrative authority as part of its activities. The extent of disclosure will again be limited by essential considerations of professional secrecy.

Where the court has attached the assets of the defendant, the sheriff's court may where the circumstances of the case, including the nature of the assets seized or the character of the defendant, warrant, place the assets under the surveillance of the court or of someone appointed by the court at the debtor's expense.

The court has power to attach debts due from third parties. The third party debtor must be informed that valid discharge of the debt can only be made to the plaintiff.

5.07. **Finland.** There are two main forms of interim protection under Finnish law: the attachment of assets and prohibitive injunctions. Application for such measures must be in writing and made to the competent court which will have jurisdiction over the main action.

Attachment of assets may be applied for *ex parte* to protect the plaintiff's claim in circumstances where there is a danger that the opposing party will conceal, destroy or transfer his assets thus endangering the plaintiff's claim. Also an object or certain property being in the custody of the opposing party may be attached if the plaintiff is able to show a prima facie case that he has a better right to the property.

A prohibitive injunction can be used to prevent the opposing party acting contrary to the plaintiff's interest. A penalty notice may be attached to the injunction.

In addition, the following interim orders are available:

(1) specific performance;
(2) that assets of the opposing party are placed in the custody of an appointed trustee; and
(3) such other measure as is necessary to preserve the plaintiff's right or interest.

Once an order for interim protection has been given it is enforced by the court bailiff. Normally the plaintiff must provide security to cover the damages which may be caused to the opposing party by the interim order. If the plaintiff has not yet commenced the main action, it must bring that action before the competent court within one month from the date of the order for interim protection.

5.08. France. Not all provisional measures are available on an *ex parte* basis. Only those fulfilling the dual requirements of urgency and secrecy may be granted *ex parte* by Ordonnances sur Requête. Other provisional measures will be granted following an *inter partes* hearing by Ordonnances de Référé. The president of the commercial court and the Juge de l'Exécution enjoy a great discretion to grant *ex parte* orders and this is not limited by precedent. There are only the two pre-conditions; namely urgency and secrecy.

The most frequent *ex parte* measures provide for the inspection of a place or documents by a bailiff, the seizure of goods or documents by a bailiff or attachment.

Four forms of provisional measures are available *ex parte*, the first two being merged in the category of sûretés judiciaires.

(1) The "inscription d'hypothèque conservatoire" is the registration of a provisional mortgage on realty belonging to the debtor, such registration being authorised *ex parte* by the court. Once the claim is confirmed on the merits by a final judgment, the mortgage will also be confirmed and take precedence as from the date of the provisional registration.

(2) The "nantissement conservatoire" works as the "inscription d'hypothèque conservatoire" but the charge is registered on the "fonds de commerce", which basically consist of the goodwill, the commercial name, and any leasehold property. It may also include the stock and the intangible assets of a business.

The other two forms of attachment consist of the Saisie Conservatoire and the Saisie Attribution.

The Saisie Conservatoire allows the plaintiff an attachment if (1) he can show evidence of a prima facie case, and (2) satisfaction of the future claim is imperilled by the risk of removal or disposal of assets by the defendant. If the plaintiff has not commenced proceedings on the merits at the time of the application, the order will require the plaintiff to initiate such proceedings.

The Saisie Attribution is granted where a creditor can establish that his claim, although not liquidated, is due and certain. Once the creditor has been authorised to effect the Saisie Attribution, he is bound to summon the debtor before the TGI so that the court may verify the formal regularity of the attachment and order the payment of the claim by transfer of the goods or monies attached. The creditor must also summon the debtor before the court with jurisdiction on the merits in order to establish title.

The powers of the presidents of the TGI, the TI, the Tribunal de Commerce or the Conseil des Prud'hommes in *inter partes* proceedings are extensive. They include the power to grant orders for:

(a) injunctions necessary for the preservation of evidence; usually the appointment of a court expert;
(b) any necessary urgent measures, not susceptible to serious legal challenge;
(c) any necessary injunctions to prevent threatened peril or stop a blatantly illegal situation;
(d) interim payment;
(e) appointment of a receiver to preserve assets under dispute, management of a company unable to muster a majority at the board or shareholder level, summoning a general meeting of shareholders.

Provisional *inter partes* orders are granted either by the President of the court sitting as juge des référés, or, if proceedings on the merits are under way, by the master (juge de la mise en état at the TGI). Proceedings before the President are begun by summons for hearing within a period ranging from 24 hours to 15 days. Before the master the party seeking the order must submit a special application.

5.09. **Germany.** Interim protection of assets is limited to two general forms of provisional measure; attachment (Arrest), and temporary injunction (einstwillige Verfügung). Attachment secures a pecuniary claim pending the outcome of the main proceedings. Otherwise all other forms of protection are achieved through the temporary injunction.

Ancillary to the two general forms of order are various particular orders. The so-called Order for Performance (Leistüngsverfügung) is an exception to the general principle that provisional relief may not grant the plaintiff full satisfaction of his claim. However, this form of relief is only available either where statute expressly provides or where the plaintiff is dependent upon immediate performance and non-performance would cause him substantial irreparable harm. Practical instances of such necessity include claims for restraint of trade in competition cases and delivery of an object to the prior owner in cases of unlawful interference.

In matrimonial disputes the temporary injunction gives way to a special form of order; namely the "einstwillige Anordnung".

5.09:1. Attachment Orders. Attachment orders are designed to ensure for the plaintiff a certain security in the event of success in the primary claim. The order may either lie against the defendant's assets or be imposed against the defendant in person. Section 933 of the Code on Civil Procedure provides that the defendant may be put in jail or other restrictions may be placed on his movements so as to limit the possibility that he could remove his assets and thereby worsen his personal financial situation. However, this order is rarely used.

In order to seek an order for attachment the claim to be secured must be capable of expression as a pecuniary claim, for example, payment of the price or monetary damages. The claim must also be subsisting at the time of the application for attachment. Application for attachment can also be made in respect of conditional claims and claims not yet due. This would include an application for security for costs.

In seeking an order for attachment, the applicant must establish the need for such an order. The order is intended solely to prevent the deterioration of the defendants' assets *vis-à-vis* the plaintiff's claim, but not to improve the plaintiff's position. Consequently, the applicant must show that without the order enforcement of the judgment would be frustrated or made more difficult. It is not sufficient to show that current circumstances threaten enforcement of a judgment at a later date if those circumstances are not expected to worsen. Factors which would be sufficient encompass conduct of the defendant and such actions of third parties, other than the enforcement of ordinary claims, as could trigger or accelerate a financial collapse of the defendant. It is recognised that the mere possibility that execution of the judgment must be carried out abroad is sufficient ground for an order for attachment. Despite the possible conflict with the terms of the Conventions, it is still the prevailing view within Germany that "foreign" begins at the international boundaries of Germany and no account should be taken of the possibility of execution under the Conventions.

An order for attachment against a person is only possible when there is no other means to secure the plaintiff's claim.

The order for attachment on real property and similar assets is implemented by registration of the charge on the assets. A special regime exists for registered ships and ships under construction.

It is possible for the defendant to have an order for attachment set aside upon payment of an appropriate amount into the local court (Hinterlegung).

An order for attachment will not be granted where the plaintiff's claim is already sufficiently secured from other sources.

5.09:2. **Temporary Injunctions.** Two types of temporary injunction exist; the securing order and the regulating order. To obtain such an order the plaintiff must simply state adequate facts and establish a sufficient legal basis for his claim. The securing order restrains the conduct of the defendant in relation to the object in dispute in order to prevent its deterioration. In contrast the regulating order aims to prevent the disruption of a subsisting legal relationship between the parties such as would lead to substantial prejudice to the plaintiff or as is necessary to prevent threatened force.

An important factor to be remembered in making any application is that an order will be denied if the application is not made within certain time limits, such that the need for urgency falls away. The time limits are set by the regional courts and vary from four weeks to six months.

Normally in civil proceedings, the court is limited to granting only such relief as is requested by the applicant. However where temporary injunctions are sought the court has a wide discretion to grant those security measures it considers necessary and sufficient.

The "Schutzschrift" is a concept which has developed outside the statutory framework. Under the provisions of the Civil Procedure Code it is possible for a temporary injunction to be issued without the defendant being heard. Accordingly it is common for a potential defendant, who fears that a motion will be filed, to lodge with the court a statement of defence, the so-called "Schutzschrift", prior to the motion for temporary injunction being filed. In this statement of defence, the potential defendant explains why any subsequent motion for the issue of a temporary injunction would not be justified in the particular matter.

5.10. Greece. The Greek courts have jurisdiction to grant an application for provisional measures even if the litigant is a foreigner. Competence of the Greek court is based upon the local jurisdiction of the court.

The Greek courts will order provisional measures where there is an urgent case or an imminent threat to the rights in dispute or the means of its satisfaction. The applicant must establish a prima facie case in his favour for his substantive claim.

General competence to grant provisional or protective measures rests with the single-member Courts of First Instance. The Court of Peace is also competent to grant provisional or protective measures, where it has jurisdiction over the substantive case. Equally the multi-member division of the Court of First Instance, the Court of Appeal and the Committal Division of the Areios Pagos have jurisdiction to grant provisional measures where the case is pending before them.

Determination of the competent civil court is made in accordance with the general rules of civil procedure governing local jurisdiction. The civil courts have the power to order provisional or protective measures even where the substantive case has been submitted to arbitration.

An application for provisional measures is begun by filing the relevant petition with the competent court. The petition constitutes the originating process and must comply (*mutatis mutandis*) with the same requirements as the originating process for a substantive action. It should also explain the need for the provisional measures and contain a request for such measures. Only in very urgent cases will the hearing be *ex parte*.

At the hearing the procedure is oral and the witnesses are examined in court. After the hearing and within the period set by the judge, usually two working days, the parties attend with their written briefs and all documents and evidence in support of their case.

The court has a complete discretion as to the provisional measures it may grant and is not restricted to ordering the measure requested by the applicant. Where more than one measure is available, the court should order the measure which will be least burdensome to the defendant.

An applicant may be required to put up security for any measures granted. Further, if substantive proceedings have not been begun, the court may require them to be issued within a set period, usually 30 clear days from the date of the judgment issued, otherwise the measure is automatically lifted.

The forms of provisional measures are set out in an exclusive list in the Code on Civil Procedure. The most important are the following:

5.10:1. Prenotation of a Mortgage. Prenotation of a mortgage is possible against immoveable property belonging to the defendant. This remedy effectively provides a right in rem, in as much as, when the prenotation is converted into a full mortgage (for example on final judgment), the charge on the property is deemed to take effect from the date of the registration of the prenotation.

5.10:2. The Saisie Conservatoire. The most commonly used measure, the saisie conservatoire, is available against moveable and immoveable property belonging to the defendant, whether in his control or temporarily in the possession of third parties. This form of order can be used both against property of the defendant in the hands of a third party, and also against debts or claims owed by the third party to the defendant.

The saisie conservatoire is granted in respect of monetary claims and is effected by service of the order upon the defendant and the attachment of the assets by the court bailiff.

Due to the laws governing bank secrecy, it is almost impossible to invoke a saisie conservatoire against a bank account.

5.10.3. Provisional Accommodation. The court has a general power to order such interim measures as may seem appropriate. The most important cases falling within this category are those concerning the possession or tenancy of land or other immovable property. Given the sensitivity of such cases, there is an exceptional right of appeal against judgments relating to provisional measures in cases dealing with the possession or tenancy of land.

Although there is no general process of discovery between the parties in the course of litigation, it is possible through this form of order to compel third parties to disclose documents to an interested litigant. There is no special provision for forcing disclosure of a bank's books, but an applicant can seek disclosure from a bank through this measure subject to the rules of confidentiality which govern banks.

5.10:4. Judicial Sequestration. Where there is a dispute about the ownership, possession or tenancy of moveables or immoveables the court has the power to grant a provisional sequestration order. The extent of this power is such that it covers sequestration of commercial samples, books, documents, samples and specimens, provided the petitioner is entitled to the disclosure or delivery-up of such items under the substantive law. The forms of order available to the court extend to the appointment of receivers to enter in and preserve assets.

5.10:5. Public Deposit. There are no provisions for the payment of money into court. However, the court has the power to order the deposit of money, and other items capable of being deposited, with the Loan and Deposits Fund.

5.10:6. Revocation etc. of Provisional Measures. Save in disputes over possession, there is no right of appeal from a decision concerning the grant or refusal of provisional measures. However, should there be a change of circumstances, the court which ordered the provisional measures has the power to revoke, alter or modify its order at any time up to the first hearing of the principal or substantive case. After the first hearing only the court dealing with the substantive case may revoke, modify or impose a provisional measure.

5.11. Ireland. The Irish courts have a power to grant a Mareva Injunction in similar circumstances and according to similar principles as those applying in the courts in England and Wales.

The same comment applies in respect of an Anton Piller Order. However, such orders are infrequent and an applicant bears a burden of proof to establish a strong prima facie case which is greater than the normal standard of civil proof. In order to obtain the order, the applicant will have to give strict undertakings to the court. There has been academic comment that such an order may conflict with certain constitutional rights in respect of property.

The court has power to appoint a receiver for the protection and preservation of assets, but it is a power which is not commonly used. In similar vein, the court can grant orders for the detention, preservation or inspection of any property or thing.

Orders for payment into court are possible. It is, however, more usual for monies to be held jointly by the parties or to be held by a third party such as a bank.

5.12. Italy. Provisional measures are designed to maintain the status quo pending a final decision. Generally such measures will be begun *ex parte* and be followed by an *inter partes* hearing. Potential measures available to parties include attachment and temporary injunctions.

Attachment orders are either judicial or protective. A judicial order is granted by the court in order to provide for enforcement of the claim, or the protection of evidence. A protective order attaches to the defendant's assets and is intended to secure the plaintiff's claim. For both forms of order the procedure is the same. When an action is already pending, the application is made to that court. Otherwise the application is made to the Pretore or Chairman of Tribunal having financial jurisdiction for the area where attachment is to be effected.

Where assets are attached, the judge will appoint a sequestrator to hold the assets and can ask the applicant to provide a cross-security in the form of an indemnity against damages and expenses.

Enforcement of the order requires the party seeking attachment to serve the order on the other party. At this moment, possession of the assets attached will transfer either to the applicant or to a third party.

Where no proceedings on the merits are under way, the applicant must notify the fact of attachment to the respondent within 15 days of the order being made. The notice must indicate the items upon which attachment was made and further summon the respondent to an *inter partes* hearing before the court having jurisdiction in the main action to confirm the attachment order and begin proceedings on the main claim. Where the Italian courts do not have jurisdiction to make a decision on the merits, the summons has to be brought before the court which granted the original order for attachment, which court will make a final order.

Interlocutory injunctions take two forms. The judge may make an order restraining damage reasonably expected to result to the applicant from new works or otherwise believed to be serious or impending. The judge has a wide discretion as to the form of order he may make in order to prevent damage occurring.

The other form of order is more general and provides the court with a wide discretion to grant such urgent measures as it thinks appropriate in order to secure the applicant's position following a decision on the merits.

5.13. Luxembourg. Under the Civil Code of Luxembourg there is provision for interim protection through the vehicles of the Saisie–Arrêt, Saisie–Conservatoire and the Saisie–Gagèrie. The Saisie–Gagèrie is a measure reserved for litigation between a landlord and a tenant following non-payment of rent. The order allows the landlord to attach all the moveable goods of the tenant which are on the rented premises.

The Saisie–Arrêt attaches to goods of a debtor in the hands of a third party. When the creditor has not already established title to the goods, he must seek an order from the President of the district court. Such an order will be *ex parte* in the first instance. Once the order has been served by the bailiff, the debtor is informed thereof and may return to court to set the order aside. On the other side, the creditor has to begin proceedings on the merits to resolve his entitlement to the amount claimed and to validate his right to the attachment. If he succeeds, the goods may be sold for his benefit.

The Saisie–Conservatoire is a measure available in commercial matters to a creditor allowing him to attach the goods of a debtor upon the order of the President of the commercial court. The attached goods may be sold once the creditor has established an enforceable title.

5.14. The Netherlands. Provisional measures in the Netherlands primarily consist of attachments and injunctions.

The Conservatoir Beslag is the equivalent of the Mareva Injunction. It will be granted where there is good reason to presume that the debtor may seek to dispose of his assets before judgment. Initial application is on an *ex parte* basis to the President of the Arrondissementsrechtsbank and, where appropriate, before the main proceedings in respect of the claim have been started. Normally, no security is required from the creditor.

If the application is made before the main proceedings have been started, a period of at least eight days will be set within which the main proceedings are to be started. If he does not succeed in the main proceedings the creditor will be liable to the debtor for damages in respect of any loss suffered by reason of the seizure. The debtor can seek to discharge the order either by providing alternative security or by challenging it in summary proceedings. Provisional attachment is also possible for goods or monies held by third parties but due to the debtor.

Where moveable assets in the hands of a debtor are attached, their preservation may be ensured by the appointment of a receiver (bewaarder).

There are no provisions for an order to pay money into court, but a party may seek an injunction against the defendant to pay a certain amount as an advance.

5.15. Norway. The relevant provisional measure for claims which are capable of being quantified in monetary terms is attachment of the defendant's assets ("arrest"). As far as other claims are concerned, the applicable measure is a prohibitive injunction against the defendant ("midlertidig forfoyning").

Applications for such interim measures should be filed with the local Court of Execution and Enforcement ("namsrett"), either where the defendant is domiciled or where the assets in question are located. However, if the underlying proceedings aimed at resolving the dispute between the parties has already gone beyond the stage of the Conciliation Council hearing, the application should be filed directly with the court handling the substantive proceedings.

An order for the attachment of assets may be granted if the defendant's behaviour indicates that, in the absence of such an order, enforcement or execution of the plaintiff's underlying claim will be impossible or particularly difficult or will have to take place abroad. The court will need to be satisfied that the underlying claim is reasonably justified.

A prohibitive injunction may be granted if the defendant's behaviour makes an injunction necessary in order to secure enforcement or execution of the plaintiff's underlying claim. Alternatively, an injunction may be granted if it appears from the defendant's conduct that the order will be necessary in order to prevent substantial damage, inconvenience or violence. When deciding whether to grant the injunction, the court will have to take into account any damage or inconvenience to the defendant caused by the injunction and will need to be satisfied that the underlying claim is reasonably justified.

An order for the attachment of assets prohibits the defendant from disposing of the assets in question. In exceptional circumstances the defendant may also be prohibited from leaving Norway until the proceedings have been finalised if this is considered necessary to enforce the order for the attachment of assets.

The specific wording of a prohibitive injunction may vary substantially from case to case depending on the nature of the claim. Essentially, the court may specify any reasonable measures deemed necessary to prevent the defendant from acting contrary to the plaintiff's interest.

The plaintiff may be required to post a bond with the court as security in respect of any damage suffered by the defendant as a result of the provisional measure under consideration. Such bond will have to be posted before the provisional measure is implemented.

5.16. Portugal. Provisional measures (Procedimentos Cautelares) can be sought either in the course of litigation or before the issue of proceedings. If such measures are sought before proceedings are issued, they will lapse if the substantive proceedings are not issued within 30 days from the court's order. Failure in the application for the provisional measures before the issue of substantive proceedings will not affect the issue of or decision in the substantive proceedings.

The following various provisional measures are available to a plaintiff.

5.16:1. Interim Delivery Up. This requires the plaintiff to establish three elements: original possession by the plaintiff, dispossession by the defendant and the use of force in the dispossession.

5.16:2. Suspension of Corporate Decisions. A shareholder may request the court to suspend the execution of any decision taken by a company or association in breach of its laws or byelaws if the execution of the decision will lead to considerable damage. The shareholder has five days from the date of the decision to bring his application and must produce a minute of the meeting when the decision was made.

5.16:3. Arrest. A creditor may apply for the provisional arrest of goods when there is a danger that the debtor will dissipates his assets and be unable to meet the creditor's claim. When the creditor makes his application, he must describe the facts which show his claim against the debtor, justification for his fear of the dissipation of the assets and if possible a list of the goods to be arrested.

A form of remedial arrest exists for the illegal use of industrial or commercial marks. Evidence of the existence of the industrial or commercial property rights must be produced together with evidence of the infringement of those rights. Special rules exist for applications for arrest against treasurers, receivers, debtors of the State or other public legal entities.

An application for arrest is initially made *ex parte*. Once the defendant is notified of the arrest, he can challenge it either by appeal or by interplea. The interplea is meant to allege facts that remove the grounds of the arrest, or to request that the arrest be reduced to its fair limits when it has covered more assets than necessary. As to the grounds of the appeal, they can be the nullity of the judge's decision or the violation or incorrect application of the substantive law or of the law of procedure. If the party files an interplea and does not, at the same time, appeal from the decision granting the arrest, that party may still allege in the interplea that the arrest should not have been ordered because of the absence of the necessary legal requirements.

5.16:4. Suspension of New Works. Anyone whose property rights or rights of possession are infringed as a consequence of new work or services and is either caused or threatened with damage may request the court to suspend the work or service. The application must be made within 30 days of the date from when the applicant knew of the work or service. The period of 30 days is counted from the date of knowledge of the fact that the work or service may cause damage. The applicant must satisfy the judge as to the need for the measure and, if required, provide summary evidence of the grounds for the application. The judge has a discretion to hear the works' owner if he finds it convenient.

It is initially possible for an applicant to exercise this remedy without the assistance of the court. The applicant must verbally request the works' owner to desist from the works in front of two witnesses. However, the decision must be ratified by the courts within five days.

This remedy cannot be exercised against the State in respect of works on public land.

5.16:5. Enrolment (Arrolamento). An application for enrolment can be made when someone has a justified fear of the dissipation of assets, moveable or immoveable, or of documents. The person making the application must show on summary evidence an interest in the preservation of the goods or documents and the facts upon which he can found his fear of their dissipation. The person against whom the order is to be made may be heard on the application if this would not compromise the purpose of the application.

An order for enrolment provides for the description, evaluation and deposit of the assets. The person appointed in the order to hold the assets will usually be the person already in possession.

5.16:6. Other Relief. Apart from the specific forms of relief mentioned above, the court has a general power to grant mandatory and prohibitive injunctions upon application. Applications must be supported by summary evidence of the rights under threat and the grounds for the fear of damage to be suffered. Relief is not to be ordered if the damage flowing from the order would outstrip the damage it is intended to prevent.

5.17. Spain. The most common forms of attachment are preventative in nature and designed to protect monetary debts or debts in kind. The remedy of attachment is available in respect of debts due to the debtor from third parties. If the debt is not incorporated in a title which is self-enforceable without the need for a prior judgment (bill of exchange, public deeds, etc.), creditors seeking an attachment will be requested to secure eventual damage to debtors arising from the attachment.

Application for attachment must be made to the Court of First Instance along with the formal writ of demand. If the sum at issue is less than ptas. 8,000 the application may also be made to the Court of Peace.

The order will not be enforced if at the time it is to be executed, the defendant pays or deposits the amount claimed or provides bail or a bank bond to the court.

The applicant can specify the property to be attached. If the property involved is immovable property, the charge will be noted on the Register of Property. Moveable goods may be attached by requiring them to be lodged with a receiver appointed by the court. Money, whether cash or securities, will be deposited with a bank.

Pursuant to section 1,411 of the Act of Procedure, the attachment order is subject to ratification at a declarative hearing, the summons for which must be presented within 20 business days of the date on which the attachment was ordered. All orders for preventative attachment are subject to such ratification when they are granted either prior to or independently of the substantive writ. The owner of the property attached can initiate the hearing for ratification by a summons served within the period of 10 business days from the date of the order. At the ratification hearing the debtor can oppose the validity of the order and if successful will recover damages arising from the attachment.

Apart from attachment, the court has the power to appoint receivers to protect and preserve assets, which are the subject of litigation. This is usually done by a court controlled administration, bank deposit, or storage at a warehouse.

If the court in the exercise of its powers requires one or both parties to lodge security for eventual damages, this will be provided by a judicial or bank bond deposited in the Caja General de Dépositos (Official Deposit Entity).

5.18. Sweden. An interim attachment of the defendant's assets ("kvarstad") can be directed at property and may be used either to preserve the possibility of enforcement of a claim for payment of a debt or enforcement of a title claim to specific items of personal property. In addition, it is possible to impose upon an alleged obligor an injunction which is tailored to the exigencies of a particular case. Such an injunction may, for example, prohibit the defendant from conducting certain business or undertaking certain activities. Applications for such interim measures must be made to the court which is competent to try the main proceedings of the case.

To obtain a protective interim order, the plaintiff must show that he has a prima facie case and that it may reasonably be suspected that the defendant is attempting to avoid payment of the plaintiff's claim or is otherwise making dispositions detrimental to the plaintiff's rights. The plaintiff must also provide sufficient security for any damages which the interim order may cause the defendant.

If an interim order is granted and the defendant subsequently provides security for the claim in respect of which the interim order was granted, then the court order will be revoked.

If the main proceedings have not been commenced when the provisional measures are granted, the plaintiff must, within one month from the decision regarding the provisional measures, commence the main proceedings.

5.19. Switzerland.

5.19:1. Interim Protection of Assets pending Trial. Different kinds of provisional measures are available. They aim to maintain an existing situation pending trial, either by preserving the object of litigation for execution after the final judgment or by preventing the defendant from acting in any way that would adversely affect the claimant's rights which are in dispute.

5.19:2. Procedure. The different kinds of provisional measures as well as the proceedings by which they are adopted and the courts or judges which are competent to issue such orders are regulated by the cantons in their individual Civil Procedure Codes. Differences exist, therefore, between the cantons. The question of whether a provisional measure may be ordered at all is one of federal law and, therefore, should be answered uniformly within the whole territory of Switzerland.

In the Canton of Zurich, provisional measures can be requested by the claimant pending trial. The application is decided by the court that decides on the main claim. Alternatively, if the application is urgent, it may be heard by a single judge of that court *ex parte* (the decision will then be open to review by the court if challenged by the defendant). If a trial has not been initiated, provisional measures may be requested in summary proceedings before a single judge. If provisional measures are granted in the course of summary proceedings, the claimant will be given a time limit for starting an action before the competent court. Failure to meet this time limit will result in the provisional measures being lifted.

Provisional measures may be ordered in *ex parte* proceedings if the claimant can show that the matter is urgent. The defendant is then given a time limit within which to file any challenge. If a challenge is filed, the first order has to be reviewed in *inter partes* proceedings and will then either be confirmed, or withdrawn.

The applicant has to show a prima facie case that he has a claim against the defendant and that without the requested provisional measure he would suffer an uncurable damage. The competent court or single judge decides whether to order provisional measures. If the decision is in favour of a provisional measure, the court also has to decide on the kind of measure to be imposed, applying the principle of proportionality ("Verhaeltnismaessigkeitsprinzip"), *i.e.* it has to order the measure that is most effective but least burdensome on the defendant. The applicant can be ordered to post security in advance for any damages which may be unjustly suffered by the defendant as a result of the interim measure.

The provisional measures can be changed any time pending trial on the application of one of the parties. Otherwise they remain in force until final judgment. At the time of giving final judgment, the court can also order that the provisional measures should stay in effect until the judgment has been enforced.

5.19:3. Provisional measures in support of a judgment for a non-monetary claim. The following provisional measures may be ordered to ensure the future enforcement of a judgment in a non-monetary claim.

If the litigation concerns moveable property, then the actual holder of the property (the defendant or a third party) can be ordered, under threat of fine and/or imprisonment, not to dispose of the property pending trial. Alternatively, the holder may be ordered to hand the property to the court where it will be kept pending trial.

In a case concerning immoveable property, the owner of the property may be prevented from changing the legal status of the property by an entry into the cantonal property register to that effect.

If the claim is to restrain a defendant from performing a specific act, then the claimant can request a temporary restraining order.

During proceedings for the liquidation of a corporate body, it may be necessary to take provisional measures to ensure the proper management of the company pending hearing. The court may then order the measures it deems necessary, the strongest measure being the appointment of a receiver.

Provisional measures are often used in intellectual property litigation, most often in the form of prohibitory injunctions.

5.19:4. Provisional measures to support a judgment for a monetary claim. Provisional measures, for example freezing the defendant's assets, to support the enforcement of a judgment for a monetary claim are only available under very restricted circumstances. Only the measures provided by the

Federal Act on Debt Collection and Bankruptcy (DCB) are available, *i.e.* attachment and provisional seizure.

The attachment of the defendant's assets will only be granted, if one of the following reasons can be established:

(1) the defendant has no domicile (whether in Switzerland or abroad);
(2) the defendant makes preparations to leave the jurisdiction or starts to set aside and hide away assets;
(3) the defendant is on his way through Switzerland and the claim by its nature has to be honoured instantly;
(4) the defendant has no domicile in Switzerland;
(5) the claimant has suffered a loss in previous debt collection or bankruptcy proceedings against the defendant.

A creditor who wants to have the assets of his debtor attached, has to show the single judge at the place of attachment (*i.e.* the place where the assets are located) prima facie evidence that he has a valid claim, and that one of the above reasons for granting the order is applicable. Furthermore, he has to name the assets to be attached and their exact location. Mere "fishing expeditions" are not tolerated. Finally, the applicant will generally be ordered to provide security for any damages that may result from an unjustified attachment. Attachments are ordered in *ex parte* proceedings. If the attachment is granted, the applicant is given a time limit within which to start proceedings in support of his claim.

Provisional seizure of the defendant's assets is only possible in one situation: namely when the creditor is (a) in possession of a signed acknowledgment of debt by the debtor, (b) has obtained, on the strength of such acknowledgment, the provisional admission of the debt in the course of debt collection proceedings, and (c) the debtor has not paid in the sum due within the time limit set in the payment order by the debt collection office.

CHAPTER 6

THE ESTABLISHMENT OF JURISDICTION

6.01. Introduction. We have seen in Chapter 1 that the Conventions seek to create a common regime for the circumstances in which a party domiciled in one contracting State may be sued in another.

The basic rule is that the defendant should be sued where he is domiciled but the exceptions to that rule cover many situations that commonly arise in an international context. The Conventions leave to domestic procedural systems the precise requirements for the local courts to invoke jurisdiction over a non-domiciliary.

All that the Conventions seek to do is to impose boundaries at the outer edges of the differing domestic regimes. Some particularly exorbitant forms of jurisdiction are expressly vetoed by Article 3 of the Conventions so as to exclude their effect against domiciliaries of contracting States, and, for some limited purposes, exclusive jurisdiction may be conferred on the courts of a particular State. As long as the domestic systems do not trespass on those boundaries, the circumstances in which they may assume jurisdiction are wide and hence the potential for local variations relatively unrestricted.

In this chapter we look at some of the basic local rules for a court assuming jurisdiction including those developed for circumstances where the Convention does not apply because the defendant is not a domiciliary of a contracting State. In reviewing the different local systems, the reader should bear in mind the restrictions which the Convention imposes, more fully described in Chapter 1.

It is important to emphasise that the only grounds upon which a question of jurisdiction between the courts of contracting States may be settled are those within the Conventions. Any other basis of jurisdiction mentioned in this chapter will only be relevant as between the contracting State concerned and non-contracting States.

Where an action arises to which the Conventions apply, the court seised with the action is required to examine of its own motion whether it has jurisdiction.

6.02. England and Wales. Where the Conventions as embodied in the amended Civil Jurisdiction and Judgments Act 1982 apply, the courts are bound by the rules of jurisdiction contained therein. In other cases, the question of jurisdiction is one for the discretion of the court. The Act also contains the rules for the division of jurisdiction between the various constituent parts of the United Kingdom.

Outside the Conventions the courts will have jurisdiction over any person who is properly served with proceedings while he is in England and Wales, even though he may be only temporarily present in the jurisdiction. Equally, the courts will have jurisdiction over any person who agrees to the jurisdiction or is deemed to have submitted to it. Acknowledgment of the service of proceedings without contesting jurisdiction will be sufficient to found the jurisdiction of the courts. A foreign plaintiff who begins proceedings in England and Wales impliedly consents to its jurisdiction in respect of any counterclaim in related matters.

In addition there are prescribed circumstances where the courts will assume jurisdiction in personam either as a matter of discretion or, in limited circumstances, as of right. In summary, discretionary jurisdiction will be adopted under the applicable rules of court whenever:

(1) relief is sought against a person domiciled in the jurisdiction;
(2) an injunction is sought ordering the defendant to do or refrain from doing anything within the jurisdiction;
(3) the claim is brought against a person duly served within or out of the jurisdiction and a person out of the jurisdiction is a necessary or proper party thereto;
(4) the claim is brought to enforce, rescind, dissolve, annul or otherwise affect a contract, or to recover damages or obtain other relief in respect of the breach of a contract, being a contract:
 (a) made within the jurisdiction, or
 (b) made by or through an agent trading or residing within the jurisdiction on behalf of a principal trading or residing out of the jurisdiction, or
 (c) by its terms, or by implication, governed by English law, or
 (d) containing a term to the effect that the High Court/County Court shall have jurisdiction to hear and determine any action in respect of the contract;
(5) the claim is brought in respect of a breach committed within the jurisdiction of a contract made within or out

of the jurisdiction and irrespective of the fact, if such be the case, that the breach was preceded or accompanied by a breach committed out of the jurisdiction that rendered impossible the performance of so much of the contract as ought to have been performed within the jurisdiction;

(6) the claim is founded on a tort and the damage was sustained or resulted from an act committed within the jurisdiction;

(7) the whole subject-matter of the action is land situate within the jurisdiction (with or without rents or profits) or the perpetuation of testimony relating to land so situate;

(8) the claim is brought to construe, rectify, set aside or enforce an act, deed, will, contract or obligation or liability affecting land situate within the jurisdiction;

(9) the claim is made for a debt secured on immoveable property or is made to assert, declare or determine proprietary or possessory rights, or rights of security, in or over moveable property or to obtain authority to dispose of moveable property, situate within the jurisdiction;

(10) the claim is brought to execute the trusts of a written instrument being trusts which ought to be executed according to English law and of which the person to be served with the writ is a trustee, or for any relief or remedy which might be obtained in any such action;

(11) the claim is for the administration of an estate of a person who died domiciled within the jurisdiction or for any relief or remedy which might be obtained in any such action;

(12) the claim is brought in a probate action within the meaning of the Rules of the Supreme Court, Order 76/County Court Rules, Order 41;

(13) the claim is brought to enforce any judgment or arbitral award;

(14) the claim is brought against a defendant not domiciled in Scotland or Northern Ireland in respect of a claim by the Commissioners of the Inland Revenue for or in relation to any of the duties or taxes which have been, or are for the time being, placed under their care or management;

(15) the claim is brought under the Nuclear Installations Act 1965 or in respect of contributions under the Social Security Act 1975;

(16) the claim is for a sum to which the Directive of the Council of the European Communities dated March 15,

1976 No. 76/308 applies and service is to be effected in a country which is a Member State of the European Economic Community;[1]
(17) the claim is made under the Drug Trafficking Offences Act 1986;
(18) the claim is made under the Financial Services Act 1986 or the Banking Act 1987;
(19) the claim is made under Part VI of the Criminal Justice Act 1988;
(20) the claim is brought for money had and received or for an account or other relief against the defendant as a constructive trustee and the defendant's alleged liability arises out of acts committed, whether by him or otherwise, within the jurisdiction.

Apart from the above discretionary grounds for exercising jurisdiction there are also various specialised enactments which give the courts jurisdiction as of right, whether or not the person concerned is within or without the jurisdiction.

In addition to its *in personam* jurisdiction, the Court also has an *in rem* Admiralty jurisdiction. This is exercised in specific circumstances, largely defined by statute, against a ship, freight, cargo or other property subject to an admiralty claim and within the jurisdiction.

Note
1. The text of the relevant rule continues to refer to The European Economic Community.

6.03. Scotland. As in England and Wales, the courts are bound by the rules of the jurisdiction in the Conventions where it applies. However, unlike England, the Scottish internal rules of jurisdiction, and the rules which govern defenders domiciled outside the United Kingdom, are also based largely on the Conventions, subject to several modifications. In general, a defender domiciled outside the contracting States may be sued in Scotland in accordance with the following rules:

(1) Where the defender has no fixed residence, when he is personally cited within Scotland;
(2) where moveable property belonging to the defender has been arrested within Scotland or where any immoveable property in which he has a beneficial interest is situated in Scotland;

(3) in proceedings which are brought to assert, declare or determine proprietary rights or rights of security over moveable property which is situated in Scotland;
(4) in actions of interdict where the wrong is threatened in Scotland;
(5) in actions involving a debt secured over immoveable property situated in Scotland;
(6) in proceedings having as their object the decision of an organ of a company or other legal person or of an association of a natural or legal person which has its seat in Scotland;
(7) in arbitrations conducted in Scotland or in which the procedure is governed by Scots law;
(8) in proceedings principally concerned with the registration in the United Kingdom or the validity in the United Kingdom of patents, trade marks, designs or other similar rights required to be deposited or registered.

6.04. Austria. The domestic rules governing the jurisdiction of the Austrian courts are influenced by various international conventions and the principles of international law.

Generally jurisdiction is founded on the domicile or residence of the defendant. However, there are various special rules giving other courts jurisdiction. Jurisdiction for claims against companies rests primarily with the court for the judicial district where the company has its seat. In the event that the company has several subsidiary offices, jurisdiction may be founded either where the company has its head office or at the location of the subsidiary office involved in the suit.

The Austrian courts will assume jurisdiction over a defendant based on his temporary residence within the jurisdiction. Jurisdiction will then rest with the court for the judicial district where the defendant has his current place of residence. In certain circumstances, if a defendant no longer has a place of residence within Austria, jurisdiction may be given to the court where the defendant had his most recent domicile or place of business.

Particular rules of jurisdiction include the following:

(1) consumers may be sued at their place of work;
(2) litigation regarding probate proceedings is subject to the jurisdiction of the court where the probate proceedings are pending;
(3) litigation regarding immovables and assets is subject to the jurisdiction of the court where the immovables and

assets are located;
(4) persons liable for unlawful acts committed by means of pamphlets or other printed matter or by any other objects mailed from abroad may be sued in the court having jurisdiction over the judicial district where the objects were delivered;
(5) persons liable on a bill of exchange may be sued in the court with jurisdiction over the place where payment was to be made;
(6) tortious claims for personal injury or damage to property may be brought in the court with jurisdiction over the place where the harmful event occurred;
(7) proprietary claims against persons who are not otherwise subject to general Austrian jurisdiction may be filed at any court with jurisdiction over the judicial district where the assets of such person or the subject matter of the dispute is located.;
(8) subject to certain limited exceptions, parties may agree to Austrian jurisdiction. The agreement must be evidenced in writing.

6.05. Belgium. The Belgian courts assume jurisdiction over parties not domiciled in Belgium or another contracting State, in circumstances prescribed in the judicial code.

The relevant circumstances can be briefly summarised:
(1) immoveable property matters;
(2) the party concerned either has a residence in Belgium or has made an election of domicile; residence is defined as any establishment or place other than domicile, where a person has a commercial or industrial establishment; elected domicile is a fictitious domicile created by the exercise of a party's will;
(3) the obligation in dispute was created in Belgium or Belgium is the place of performance;
(4) the presence of testamentary estate in Belgium;
(5) the validity or discharge of provisional measures granted in Belgium;
(6) the claim is linked to a claim already pending before the Belgian court;
(7) enforcement in Belgium of a court decision rendered or a court deed executed in a foreign country;
(8) bankruptcy proceedings in Belgium;
(9) interpleader/counterclaim in respect of a claim already pending in Belgium;

(10) there are several co-defendants, one or more of whom has his domicile or residence in Belgium;
(11) certain maritime cases in limited circumstances.

If the jurisdiction of the Belgian courts over the defendant is not determined by the above, the plaintiff may sue before the judge of the district where he has his domicile or residence. Actions against Belgian citizens in respect of obligations incurred abroad can always be begun in Belgium, even by a foreign national.

The provisions of the Belgian civil and judicial codes which provide for these bases of jurisdiction are, however, excluded in relation to domiciliaries of contracting States by Article 3 of the Brussels Convention.

Provided that reciprocal provisions exist for Belgian citizens in his country, a foreign defendant can challenge the jurisdiction of the Belgian courts in his first pleadings. A foreign defendant who does not appear before the Belgian courts will be presumed to have waived any objections to their jurisdiction.

6.06. Denmark. Actions may be begun against persons, companies, associations, private institutions and other societies or institutions for whom there is no "competent court" under the Danish Law on Civil Procedure, provided that a court may be deemed to be the appropriate venue under the relevant legislative provisions. In the first instance the "competent court" is the local court with jurisdiction for the area where the defendant is domiciled or resident, alternatively for the area of the defendant's last known domicile or address.

For businesses of any sort, jurisdiction in matters concerning the business will rest with the local court for the area where the business is carried out. Normally business will be carried out for the purposes of establishing jurisdiction at the place of management, where the mail is received and agreements signed.

Proceedings concerning interests in immoveable property may be begun at the court having jurisdiction over the district where the property is situated. This provision covers all forms of interest in the immoveable property. There is also provision for matters relating to the performance of an agreement to be heard before the court with jurisdiction for the place of performance. However, this will not apply to claims for the payment of money under a contract, unless the obligation to pay had to be fulfilled before leaving the place.

Actions for damage or the violation of rights arising from tortious and other non-contractual acts may be heard by the local court for the area where the act took place.

Alternatively it is open to the parties to agree the court to have jurisdiction. Ordinarily the agreement is binding upon both parties and should be made before any possible dispute arises. Alternatively such an agreement may also be made after the action has been commenced if the defendant is prepared to appear before the court without contesting the jurisdiction of the court.

In property cases where no other basis for jurisdiction exists, proceedings may be begun against a defendant wherever he is residing at the time the writ is served. Otherwise the jurisdiction of a local court may also be founded by the presence of assets belonging to the defendant within the jurisdiction.

If proceedings are issued before a court which is not the proper venue for the claim, the court may refer the case to a court which does have jurisdiction. However, such reference will only cover the territory governed by the Law on Civil Procedure; this does not include the Faroe Islands or Greenland.

6.07. **Finland.** Where the Lugano Convention does not apply the Finnish courts will have jurisdiction over cases involving foreigners if the foreigner has a residence and domicile in Finland. The main rule, with regard to individuals, is that the defendant may be sued where he is domiciled and, with regard to an incorporated business, where it is registered. In addition, a non-resident foreigner may be sued in Finland in the place where he is apprehended or where he has property.

Jurisdiction in matters where the defendant is incorporated, may also rest with the court for the district where the business is carried on. Actions in respect of interest in real estate are heard by the local court for the district where the property is situated. In inheritance matters jurisdiction rests with the court for the district in which the deceased person was last domiciled.

The parties may in most cases agree on the court to have jurisdiction. Such an agreement must be in writing. If the action has already commenced in another court than that which should have jurisdiction then, subject to the defendant's consent, the action may be heard in that court.

6.08. **France.** The French courts are entitled to exercise jurisdiction over parties domiciled outside France pursuant to the rules laid down in their Nouveau Code de Procédure Civile.

Actions for the recovery of immoveable property and the cancellation or performance of a deed conveying real property belong to the court having jurisdiction over the district where the property is located. In probate matters, jurisdiction belongs to the court of the last domicile of the deceased person. Issues of tortious liability may be adjudicated by the court of the place of the harmful event or alternatively the place where the ensuing loss occurs. Issues of contractual liability may be decided by the court with jurisdiction over the place of delivery or over the place of performance of the service which is contractually due.

Under the rules governing bankruptcy, members of the board of a bankrupt company may be personally sued before the court for the place of the registered office of the company.

Apart from jurisdiction determined by the subject-matter of the claim, jurisdiction may also be granted by the nationality of the parties. A French citizen may sue a foreigner, not resident in France, before the French courts in any matter except for the recovery of immoveable property not located in France. Equally a foreigner may sue a French citizen before the French courts in any matter except for the recovery of immoveable property not located in France. These provisions of French civil procedure are, however, expressly excluded from operating as regards domiciliaries of contracting States by Article 3 of the Conventions.

6.09. **Germany.** The German law of civil procedure is governed by the principle that the plaintiff follows the defendant; the general rule being that the plaintiff has to bring a suit where the defendant can be found.

Apart from jurisdiction established by the residence or domicile of the defendant, the German courts also have jurisdiction in the following cases:

(1) where the defendant has assets in Germany, even if those assets are not connected to the matter in issue;
(2) when the subject of the dispute is situate in Germany; this jurisdiction is exclusive for landlord and tenant disputes;
(3) when the place of performance of the contract is located in Germany;
(4) when the tortious act is committed in Germany, regardless of the place where injury occurs;
(5) in any case, if the defendant enters an appearance without contesting the jurisdiction of the court;
(6) by agreement between the parties; however, lower courts may decline jurisdiction if sufficient nexus is not established between the matter in dispute and Germany.

6.10. Greece. A Greek court will have jurisdiction over a matter whether the litigants are Greek or foreign nationals or citizens, if it has geographic competence under Greek law to hear the case. The issue of jurisdiction is a question the court must examine of its own motion.

The basic element establishing the competence of the relevant local court is the domicile of the defendant. A person's domicile is the place where he has his principal and permanent establishment. If that person carries on business, he will have a special domicile at his place of business for matters affecting that business. The jurisdiction over legal persons with the capacity to be litigants is determined by their seat of activity.

If a person does not have a domicile in Greece, then jurisdiction may be established by reference to his place of residence, or failing that, his last known domicile or residence.

For contractual claims, a concurrent jurisdiction is vested in the court for the place where the contract was or was to be performed, alternatively the place where the agreement was completed may provide a basis for the courts to take jurisdiction. Proprietary claims, whether in respect of moveable or immoveable property, may be begun before the court where the defendant has assets or where the object of the dispute is located.

A concurrent jurisdiction granted to the court for the place where the tortious act occurred only arises if the tortious act in question is one which constitutes a criminal offence. The concept of commercial domicile allows jurisdiction to be established over a company wherever the company has a branch, an agency, a representative office or other similar establishment.

Procedurally, any court which has competence over one of several defendants will also have jurisdiction over the other defendants. Further, once a court has jurisdiction over the main case, it will have an exclusive jurisdiction over any collateral proceedings, including third party proceedings. The court with jurisdiction over the main action will have a concurrent jurisdiction over any counterclaim; the counterclaim does not have to be related to the facts or circumstances of the main action.

The competent Greek court will have exclusive jurisdiction over actions concerning:

(1) rights in immoveable property situate in its area;
(2) the relationship between a company with its seat in the court's area and the shareholders or partners or quotaholders;

(3) disputes arising from the dissolution and liquidation of a company with its seat in the court's area and the distribution of its assets, provided the action is begun within two years of the completion of the distribution.

Save where Greek law provides for a competent court to have exclusive jurisdiction over a proprietary interest, it is possible for the parties to enter a binding agreement for choice of jurisdiction. This agreement does not have to be in writing, unless it is intended to apply to future disputes between the parties. If the parties seek to avoid the exclusive jurisdiction of the court, the agreement must be express.

Save where the defendant tacitly or expressly accepts the jurisdiction of the particular local court, that court is under an obligation to examine of its own motion the question of its own material and geographic competence.

6.11. Ireland. Outside the Conventions the Irish courts will generally have jurisdiction if the defendant can be properly served with the proceedings in Ireland; this may arguably extend to service during a fleeting visit to Ireland[1].

Submission to the jurisdiction to the Irish courts may also occur by the instruction of solicitors in Ireland to accept service; by entering an unconditional appearance to proceedings served upon a defendant; by commencing an action as plaintiff; by seeking interlocutory relief in proceedings such that it is only consistent with an intention to challenge the merits and by agreement to submit to the jurisdiction. Otherwise the Rules of the Superior Courts provide the circumstances when an application for service out of the jurisdiction may be granted. These include circumstances where:

(1) an action brought to enforce, or otherwise effect a contract, or to recover damages or other relief for or in respect of a breach of a contract:
  (a) made within the jurisdiction;
  (b) made by or through an agent trading or residing within the jurisdiction on behalf of a principal trading or residing out of the jurisdiction;
  (c) which by its terms or by implication is governed by Irish law or is one brought in respect of a breach of contract committed within the jurisdiction;
(2) an injunction is sought as to anything to be done within the jurisdiction, but only where the Irish courts have jurisdiction as to the substance of the matter;

(3) any person out of the jurisdiction is a necessary or proper party to an action properly brought against some other person duly served within the jurisdiction;
(4) the action is founded on a tort committed within the jurisdiction.

The Irish courts have a discretion to retain or refuse jurisdiction even when the conditions of the Rules of the Superior Courts are satisfied; for example if another jurisdiction were a more convenient forum.

Note
1. Excluded by Article 3 of the Conventions for EU and EFTA domiciliaries.

6.12. Italy. Italian judges will have jurisdiction over cases involving foreign nationals regardless of nationality, if:

(1) the foreign national has residence or domicile in Italy or his representative has appeared in court in the matter or accepted Italian jurisdiction. The exception to this is a dispute involving immoveable property situated abroad;
(2) the claim concerns property situated in Italy, testamentary property belonging to a deceased Italian citizen or opened for succession in Italy;
(3) the obligations under dispute have arisen or are to be enforced in Italy;
(4) the claim relates to another case pending before the Italian court or to provisional measures to be enforced in Italy or to relationships over which the Italian courts have jurisdiction;
(5) it is a case of reciprocity, when the country to which the foreign national belongs is entitled to hear claims against an Italian citizen.

The grounds of jurisdiction mentioned above can be waived by the parties. The validity of such a waiver will be recognised if it is evidenced by a written deed and relates to obligations either between foreign nationals or between a foreign national and an Italian citizen who is neither residing nor domiciled in Italy.

6.13. Luxembourg. A Luxembourg party may sue a non-resident foreigner for commitments entered into with Luxembourg nationals, even if the underlying obligations have been assumed abroad. Again Article 3 of the Conventions prevents the exercise of this jurisdiction against domiciliaries of contracting States.

The Luxembourg courts have a sole jurisdiction in respect of disputes under a contract of employment executed in Luxembourg or if the employee is a Luxembourg national.

The courts have an emergency jurisdiction for matters of urgency, for example an order for attachment, where the moveable or immoveable property is situate in Luxembourg.

6.14. The Netherlands. Outside the Conventions, parties not domiciled in the Netherlands may be sued before the court of the plaintiff's domicile.

If a party has no known domicile in the Netherlands, any assets he possesses here may be the subject of a preservation measure known as a "saisie foraine". The debtor may then be sued in the court where the measure takes effect.

6.15. Norway. In the first instance, actions may, in most cases, be commenced in the Conciliation Council or Local Court having jurisdiction over the area in which the defendant is domiciled. In relation to legal persons, actions may also be commenced in any Conciliation Council or Local Court having jurisdiction over an area in which the legal person has a place of business (*e.g.* a shop).

However, for certain types of litigation relating to a specific fixed property located in Norway, the action will have to be brought in the Conciliation Council or Local Court having jurisdiction over the area where the fixed property is situated. A Conciliation Council or Local Court may still exercise jurisdiction over cases concerning a fixed property in its area, even if it does not have a mandatory jurisdiction.

Actions related to the performance of contractual obligations may always be heard before the Conciliation Council or Local Court having jurisdiction over the place in which the obligation should have been performed according to the contract. Actions in respect of both contractual or non-contractual claims for damages may be heard before the Conciliation Council or Local Court which has jurisdiction over the place in which the plaintiff suffered the immediate loss in question, as well as before the Conciliation Council or local court having jurisdiction over the place in which the defendant carried out the actions giving rise to the liability for damages.

Actions against persons not domiciled in Norway may be brought in any Conciliation Council or Local Court having jurisdiction over a place in which an asset owned by the defendant is located. The asset in question does not need to be related to the dispute and may, for instance, include financial instruments, clothing, etc. This implies that to a large extent an individual temporarily located in Norway may be subject to legal action in the Conciliation Council or Local Court having jurisdiction over the area in which he is located at the moment. However, under Article 3 of the Lugano Convention, the provisions described in this paragraph cannot be used against domiciliaries of contracting States to the Convention.

If more than one individual or legal person is liable for a particular claim, *e.g.* as debtor(s) and guarantor(s), an action may normally be brought against all parties in the Conciliation Council or Local Court before which action may be brought against any one of them.

Whilst the above paragraphs set out the general rules on jurisdiction, specific types of cases may also be heard before other particular tribunals. Finally, subject to the mandatory requirements governing certain cases over fixed property, the parties are free to agree which Conciliation Council or Local Court should have jurisdiction. This principle also enables a party to agree that no Norwegian court should have jurisdiction over the matter at hand. Conversely, a party which would otherwise not be covered by the jurisdiction of any Norwegian court may agree to an action being brought in a Norwegian court.

6.16. Portugal. The Portuguese courts will accept jurisdiction over a matter following confirmation that:

(1) the law suit has been filed in Portugal in accordance with the rules of Portuguese law governing territorial jurisdiction; or

(2) the acts upon which the cause of action is based occurred within the Portuguese territory; or

(3) the defendant is a foreigner and the plaintiff is Portuguese, (provided that Portuguese nationals may be potential defendants before the courts of the defendant's Country)[1]; or

(4) the rights cannot be protected unless suit is filed in Portugal and there is a real/personal connection between the law suit to be filed and the Portuguese territory.

Where the court with jurisdiction under Portuguese law is the court of the defendant's domicile, the Portuguese courts may exercise jurisdiction as long as the defendant has been living in Portugal for more than six months. Additionally when the cause of action is breach of a contract with a Portuguese national, the courts will exercise jurisdiction if the defendant is by chance within Portuguese territory.

The Portuguese courts will claim exclusive jurisdiction in certain situations:

(a) actions concerning real property within the Portuguese territory;
(b) the insolvency of a corporate body with its head office in Portugal;
(c) questions of employment law.

Note
1. Subject to Article 3 of the Conventions.

6.17. Spain. Spain is party to several multilateral conventions in respect of specific matters which entrust jurisdiction to foreign courts. Among those treaties, Spain is party to the Brussels and the Lugano Conventions (see Chapter 1). There are also bilateral treaties governing enforcement of foreign judgments which provide for the jurisdiction of foreign courts indirectly by way of construction.

In the absence of applicable international treaties, the Spanish courts have an exclusive jurisdiction over issues of title and leasing concerning immovable property situated in Spain; over the constitution, validity, nullity or dissolution of companies or juridical persons domiciled in Spanish territory and in respect of resolutions and decisions of their organs.

The Spanish courts are also exclusively competent for the recognition and enforcement in Spanish territory of judicial or arbitral decisions taken abroad; for the validity or nullity of any registration carried out in a Spanish registry and for the registration or validity of patents or other rights where the deposit or registration of those rights has taken place in Spain.

The courts further have jurisdiction over the following matters:

(1) contractual disputes when Spain is the place of performance of the contract or the place where liability arose;
(2) extra-contractual liability accruing in Spain;

(3) disputes concerning moveable property located in Spain at the time the claim is made;
(4) contracts for the sale of goods by instalment or contracts for the financing of the acquisition of such goods, when the purchaser is a consumer and is domiciled in Spain;
(5) the operation of a branch, agency or mercantile establishment, when these are legally registered within the Spanish territory;
(6) Saisies Conservatoires or attachment proceedings in respect of persons or property located in Spanish territory.

6.18 Sweden. Action should as a general rule (under the Swedish Code on Judicial Procedure) be commenced in the district court within whose jurisdiction the defendant is domiciled. There are, however, several exceptions to the general rule:

(1) in respect of litigation which falls within the Lugano Convention, the rules on special jurisdiction contained in Article 2 of the Convention, apply;
(2) where disputes fall outside the ambit of the Convention, the Swedish Code on Judicial Procedure establishes jurisdiction as an alternative to the general rule, on the following basis:
   (a) in respect of contract or debt actions, the place where the contract was formed or debt incurred (if the defendant has no registered residence in Sweden);
   (b) in respect of real property disputes the place where the real property is located;
   (c) the place where activities are carried on at a permanent business establishment ("fast driftställe");
   (d) in respect of a tortious action the place where the tortious act occurred or had its impact;
   (e) the place where a person temporarily resides if he has incurred a debt at that place;
   (f) the location of the property belonging to a defendant with no residence in Sweden;
   (g) the place where the court has given judgement and the dispute concerns the litigation costs.

Further provisions exist for establishing jurisdiction in specific cases. The parties to a dispute may agree on a competent court as long as the agreement is not contrary to mandatory requirements regarding exclusively competent courts, such as courts which decide disputes on real property.

6.19. Switzerland. Where the Lugano Convention is not applicable, the Swiss courts will decide their jurisdiction in international matters pursuant to the provisions of the Federal Act on Private International Law (PIL).

In general, the Swiss courts will accept jurisdiction, if the defendant has his domicile, habitual residence, or its seat in Switzerland. This general rule applies to claims concerning contractual obligations in general (Art. 112, para. 1, PIL), including intellectual property rights, consumer and employee contracts, claims based on unjust enrichment (ungerechtfertigte Bereicherung) (Art. 127, PIL) and claims based on tort (unerlaubte Handlung) (Art. 129, para. 1, PIL) as well as claims based on company law (Art. 151, para. 1, PIL).

Further to this primary jurisdiction, the PIL also provides for different alternative or additional places of jurisdiction for specific types of claim. Such alternative places of jurisdiction include:

(1) for claims of the consumer (based on a consumer contract as defined in Art. 120, para. 1, PIL) the Swiss courts at the domicile or habitual residence of a claimant consumer (incidentally, this place of jurisdiction cannot be waived by the consumer in advance);

(2) for claims by an employee under an employment contract, the place of the employee's domicile or habitual residence, or the place where the employee normally carries out his work.

The PIL acknowledges some specific jurisdictions in cases where the defendant has neither domicile, nor habitual residence or seat (or branch office) in Switzerland:

(a) article 113, PIL, provides for the jurisdiction of the Swiss courts at the place of performance of a contract;

(b) article 129, para. 2, PIL, states that the Swiss courts at the place where the tortious act or the injury took place shall have jurisdiction over claims based on tort;

(c) claims concerning intellectual property rights can be brought before the courts at the place where protection against infringements is sought (Art. 109, para. 1, PIL);

(d) claims concerning rights over immoveable property have to be brought before the courts at the place where the real estate is located Art. 97, PIL).

Claims concerning moveable property can be brought before the courts at the place where the property in dispute is located, if the defendant has neither domicile, nor habitual residence in Switzerland (Art. 98, para. 2, PIL).

Finally, Swiss courts will assume jurisdiction if the parties have agreed upon the jurisdiction of the Swiss courts. The agreed court cannot deny its jurisdiction when either one of the involved parties has his domicile, habitual residence or branch office in the canton of the agreed court, or when the litigation is subject to Swiss law according to the provisions of the PIL (Art. 5, para. 3, PIL). As far as contractual claims are concerned, this will always be the case when the parties have not only agreed on the jurisdiction of a Swiss court but also on the application of Swiss law to the litigation.

In pecuniary matters a Swiss court will have jurisdiction if the defendant enters an unconditional appearance and the court cannot deny jurisdiction according to Article 5, para. 3, PIL, *i.e.* if either one of the parties has its domicile, habitual residence, or branch office in the canton of the court, or if Swiss law has to be applied to the suit.

If according to the PIL no other Swiss court has jurisdiction (Art. 4, PIL), then the court with jurisdiction over assets which have been attached, will have jurisdiction over an action to confirm an injunction restraining the disposal of assets.

Article 8, PIL, provides for the court which deals with the main claim to have jurisdiction over the counterclaim as well if there is a significant connection between the main claim and counterclaim. A significant connection will be assumed, if the claims are based on the same legal relationship or agreement, if there exists a close legal connection between the claims, or if the counterclaim is validly brought as a set-off to the main claim.

CHAPTER 7

THE NOTION OF DOMICILE

7.01. Introduction. Given that the starting point of the Conventions is that a party should generally be sued in the contracting State in which he is domiciled, it is necessary to understand what is meant by domicile under the various domestic systems of law which may apply.

Here again, the common law/civil law divide is apparent. The civil law systems by and large share a similar concept of domicile. The common law, however, developed a more complex notion of domicile so that for the purposes of the Conventions, both the United Kingdom and Ireland have had to introduce special rules so as to align the concept more closely with the civil law understanding.

7.02. England and Wales.

7.02:1. Natural Persons. Under section 41 of the Civil Jurisdiction and Judgments Act 1982 the question whether a natural person is domiciled in the United Kingdom for the purposes of the Conventions is answered exclusively by a cumulative two-part test. A person must be resident in the United Kingdom and the nature and circumstances of the residence must indicate a substantial connection with the United Kingdom. There is a rebuttable presumption that the second part of the test is fulfilled if the person has been resident in the United Kingdom for the last three months or more. Similar tests are used to determine in which part of the United Kingdom a person is domiciled and also to determine whether a person is domiciled in a state other than a contracting State.

Where the above rules are not applicable, a person will be considered to be domiciled in the country where he is considered under English law to have his permanent home. Under English law a person receives a domicile of origin at birth. A legitimate child born during the lifetime of his father, will take as domicile of origin the domicile of his father at the time of birth. A legitimate child not born during the lifetime of his father or an illegitimate child has as domicile of origin the domicile of his mother at the time of his birth. Thereafter any independent person may change his domicile to one of choice by the combination of residence and the absence of any present intention to leave it permanently or for an indefinite period. A dependent person will generally have a domicile which is the same as and changes with that of the person on whom he is dependent.

A person will never be without domicile, such that a domicile cannot be changed or lost without the acquisition of a new domicile or the revival of the domicile of origin.

7.02:2. Bodies Corporate. Outside the circumstances covered by the Conventions, English law defines the domicile of a body corporate as being in the country under whose law it is incorporated. However, Article 53(1) of both Conventions provides that the domicile of a corporation or other legal person is to be its "seat". The concept of the "seat" of a corporation was not one previously known in English law. Accordingly section 42 of the Civil Jurisdiction and Judgments Act defines a corporation as having its seat in the United Kingdom if:

(1) it was incorporated under the law of a part of the United Kingdom and has its registered office or some other official address in the United Kingdom; or
(2) its central management or control is exercised in the United Kingdom.

Similar rules apply for the purposes of the Act to determine the seat of corporations domiciled in other states. In this instance, there is the added proviso that the English courts will not recognise a corporation as having its seat in a contracting State if it is shown that the courts of that State would not recognise it as having its seat there.

For the purpose of proceedings concerning the validity of the constitution, the nullity or dissolution of a corporation or the decisions of its organs which are subject to the rules on exclusive jurisdiction in Article 16(2) of both Conventions, the seat of the corporation is determined under the rules in section 44 of the Civil Jurisdiction and Judgments Act 1982. The basic rule to determine the seat of a corporation is the same as that contained in section 42 of the Civil Jurisdiction and Judgments Act 1982, save that there is no requirement for the presence of a registered office or other official address in the United Kingdom. The further distinction is the provision that where a corporation is deemed to have its seat in the United Kingdom under the above rule, then it will not be considered to have its seat in any other contracting State even if formed under the law of that State or exercising its central management and control there.

7.02:3. **Trusts.** Under section 45 of the Civil Jurisdiction and Judgments Act 1982 a trust is domiciled in the United Kingdom if, and only if, it is domiciled in a part of the United Kingdom. A trust is only domiciled in a part of the United Kingdom if the system of law of that part is the system of law with which the trust has its closest and most real connection.

7.03. **Scotland.** Scots law has two different concepts of domicile. One is used as a basis for jurisdiction in terms of the Civil Jurisdiction and Judgments Act 1982, when the same rules apply as in England and Wales. The other, common law domicile, is (1) a basis for jurisdiction in matrimonial proceedings, and (2) the connecting factor in various choices of law rules.

At common law, a natural person has a single domicile at all times. He or she receives at birth a domicile of origin: if the child is legitimate this is the domicile of the child's father at the time of the birth; if the child is illegitimate, the domicile is that of the child's mother. Thereafter, a child's domicile generally changes with the domicile of the relevant parent, although special rules apply if the parents live apart. A person of full capacity may change his or her domicile voluntarily by a combination of residence in the new country of domicile and the intention to make that country his or her permanent home. Such a domicile (called a domicile of choice) may be lost by the acquisition of a new domicile of choice or by abandonment. If a domicile of choice is abandoned but no new domicile of choice is acquired, the person's domicile of origin revives.

At common law, the domicile of a group or association to which Scots law imputes legal personality, such as partnership or registered companies, is the place where it is formed or, if a registered company, the place of its registration and formal incorporation. The common law test of domicile of a group or association is still relevant as a connecting factor in determining which law applies in questions involving the group or association's existence, capacity, internal management and dissolution.

7.04. Austria. Jurisdiction generally depends on an individual's domicile, *i.e.* the location where the person has settled with the intention — either verifiable or obvious from the circumstances — of making it his permanent residence. If the person has no permanent domicile, the usual place of residence determines the jurisdiction; such usual place of residence is defined exclusively in accordance with the actual circumstances and depends on factors such as the duration and the permanence of residence as well as on other personal or business circumstances determining the permanence of a person's place of residence.

In accordance with the provisions of Austrian International Private Law, Austrian jurisdiction is applicable if sufficient activities or circumstances relating to Austria can be proven.

Corporations, co-operative societies, fund corporations, foundations and the like are subject to the jurisdiction at their respective seats; in cases of doubt, jurisdiction depends on the seat of the administration.

7.05. Belgium. The domicile of a natural person is defined as the place where a person is principally registered in the Register of Population. A certificate of domicile is appended by the bailiff to the writ of summons. The domicile of a corporation is determined on the basis of the company bye-laws as held at the Commercial Registry.

Trusts are unknown in Belgian law.

7.06. Denmark. The determination of whether someone is domiciled within Denmark begins with the concept of procedural domicile. This provides that the competent local court is the court where the defendant is residing; as a consequence more than one court may be competent to deal with the issue. The concept of domicile is also the determining factor as to whether someone is a native of Denmark. A native is a person whose ties to Denmark are as strong or stronger than his ties to another country by virtue of his residence in Denmark. In this context residence means the person's permanent home.

Under Danish law a company will be deemed to be domiciled in the country according to whose legislation it has been established and registered, if a process of registration exists. Although there are no specific rules for trusts in Denmark, it would be natural to apply the same rules as for companies.

7.07. Finland. The domicile of an individual is the place where he or she is principally registered in the Register of Population. Any person's domicile can be checked with the registration authorities. The domicile of a corporation is determined by its articles of association and its registration on the Companies' Registry.

Trusts are unknown under Finnish law.

7.08. France. Individuals are domiciled at the place which forms the centre of their activities. A company will be domiciled at the place of its registered office, unless that office is fictitious. Where the registered office is fictitious, the domicile of the company will be the actual centre of its activities.

There are no rules for the domicile of a trust.

7.09. Germany. The domicile of an individual is a person's place of residence. For companies and other legal persons, domicile depends upon the principal place of business of that person.

German law sets out a general rule that a person's place of residence is the place of actual settlement combined with an intention to make that place the centre of his life for the long term. Accordingly settlement in any area for a temporary purpose will not establish residence. Correspondingly, if the place of residence is to change, not only must the person actually leave the place, but he must also show an intent to abandon that place.

The residence of companies and other legal persons for the purposes of the Conventions is the administrative centre or the centre of management. However, companies whose articles of association provide for residence in Germany, cannot avoid that residence on the grounds that their actual centre of management is outside the country. Outside the Conventions, jurisdiction over companies and other legal persons is primarily determined by the seat arising at law or by agreement and, only in the absence of such a seat, by the place of actual management.

In determining the residence of an English trust, the courts will first consider whether the entity more closely resembles an enterprise or an estate. If the former, the court will look to the actual residence of the trust; if the latter it will be the location of the assets.

7.10. Greece. Under Greek law the domicile of an individual is that place where a person has a principal establishment and the choice of that place as his principal and permanent home. A person will not change his domicile until he has acquired a new domicile. Where the last domicile of a person cannot be proved, the place of his habitual residence is taken as his domicile.

Particular provisions exist for the determination of the domicile of certain persons serving the State, for example civil servants, and for those persons, such as minors, whose domicile is dependant upon another person.

For legal persons domicile is established by reference to their seat. The seat is situated in the place where a company has its management or control. There is an important exception to this rule: shipping companies whose registered office is taken as their seat for all purposes except for the establishment of jurisdiction (with the exception of Article 53 of the Brussels Convention).

7.11. Ireland. Outside the Conventions, an individual may be domiciled in the country in which he intends to live permanently or indefinitely. The domicile may be of origin, choice or dependency. This definition of domicile does not apply where the Conventions apply. For the purposes of the Conventions, the question of domicile is determined by the ordinary residence of the individual.

The rules to determine the domicile of a company outside the Conventions provide that a company is domiciled in the country where it is incorporated. The domicile may not subsequently be changed. Under the Conventions the domicile of a company is the place where the company has its seat. This concept of the seat of a company was one that was unknown to the Irish courts. A company will now have its seat in Ireland if it was incorporated or formed under the law of Ireland, or if its central control and management is exercised in Ireland.

Outside the Conventions, Irish law does not recognise the concept of the domicile of a trust. For the purposes of the Conventions a trust may be domiciled in Ireland, but only if the law of Ireland is the system of law with which the trust has its closest and most real connection.

7.12. Italy. The domicile of a natural person is determined by the place the person has chosen as the principal place of his affairs and interests. This has both an objective and a subjective element. There must first be a concentration of a person's affairs and interests in one place. Secondly there must then be intent by that person to maintain that concentration over the long term.

To determine the domicile of a legal person, one must look to the place where the legal person has its actual centre of business management, administration and organisation. For companies this will primarily be the location of the registered offices, irrespective of the location of assets or production. Trusts are a concept unknown to Italian law and accordingly there are no special rules to establish their domicile.

7.13 Luxembourg. The domicile of a natural person is the place where the individual has its main activities. This place will be determined by the individual and declared at the local registry.

The domicile of a company is the place where it has its main business.

7.14. The Netherlands. The domicile of a natural person is his place of principal residence, or, in the absence of such residence, at the place where he is actually staying. In practice, this will be the place where a person has been registered in the local civil register.

A legal person has its domicile at the place deemed to be its seat under statute, or under its articles of association or constitution. A natural or legal person with an office or branch also has domicile at that place for matters relating thereto.

7.15. Norway. An individual is domiciled at the place where he is resident. If a person maintains a residence in a place, he may be domiciled there even though he has been absent from such place for a substantial period of time. A person may be domiciled in more than one place at a time, if he maintains a residence in several different locations at any given time.

Companies and other legal persons will be domiciled at their business address as registered with the Norwegian Registry of

Companies. A legal person not registered with the said Registry will be domiciled where its board of directors or any corresponding body is convened or, if not convened, was last convened. If no such domicile can be located, a legal person will be deemed to have the same domicile as the individual on whom any petition or writ against the legal person in question is to be served, *e.g.* the chairman of the board of directors.

7.16. Portugal. If the domicile of the individual defendant is the criterion for deciding the jurisdiction of the court, domicile will be determined upon the basis of six months residence within Portuguese territory or alternatively, if the defendant has contracted with a Portuguese national, upon accidental presence in Portuguese territory.

If the defendant has his domicile and residence in a foreign country, he will be sued in the court of the place where he happens to be. Alternatively if he is not on Portuguese territory, he must be sued in the court of the domicile of the plaintiff. If the domicile of the plaintiff is also a foreign country, the Court of Lisbon will have jurisdiction.

Foreign corporations will be considered domiciled in Portugal if they have a branch, agency or delegation in Portugal. The branch, agency or delegation can both sue and be sued.

7.17. Spain. Under Spanish law "domicile" forms the key criterion ("fuero") in order to determine which court is to adjudicate within the Spanish territory (see Chapter 2) in the absence of submission by the parties to the dispute or other rules of law.

The most important of the rules for determining domicile within Spain in civil and commercial matters in the absence of conventions introducing rules of domicile are set out below:

(1) The legal domicile of businessmen for mercantile acts or agreements is the town in which their commercial operations are located. If they have establishments in different districts, they may be sued in a district other than that of their main establishment. Alternatively, the businessman may be sued in the district where his obligations have been contracted.

(2) The domicile of civil and mercantile companies will be the town stated in the deed of incorporation or bye-laws, and, if not so stated therein, will be the same as for

businessmen. In the case of Stock Companies, domicile will be the place where administration and management of the main establishment or operation is centred. In this last case the place of domicile will be shown on the official register.
(3) The domicile of legal persons is the place where their legal representation or their main function is located or as determined in their Deeds of Constitution or bye-laws.
(4) The domicile of employees is the town where they exercise their functions or where they live most frequently.
(5) The domicile of diplomats who reside abroad will be their last domicile in Spanish territory.

Apart from these rules, the Civil Code provides that in order to exercise rights and fulfil obligations, the domicile of individuals will be that of their usual residence.

When the competent court is to be determined by domicile and the person to be summoned is not domiciled in Spanish territory, competence will fall upon the court of the place of temporary residence. Those who have no current temporary residence and those who have no stable residence may be summoned before the court of the place where they are momentarily staying or the court of their last known residence, at the discretion of the claimant.

7.18. **Sweden.** A natural person is domiciled in the municipality where his civil registration was on November 1, of the preceding year. A person who has no known registered residence either within or outside Sweden is considered domiciled where he has his habitual residence.

A company, an association or a foundation ("stiftelse") is considered domiciled in the municipality where the board of directors has its registered office or, if there is no such registered office or in the absence of a board of directors, where its administration is located. A limited company ("aktiebolag") registers its board of directors with the registration authority ("Patent och registreringsverket").

7.19. **Switzerland.** In Switzerland there exist two notions of domicile, one according to the Swiss Civil Code for the purpose of purely national matters, and another one according to the Swiss Federal Act on Private International Law ("PIL") for the purpose of international matters. The notion of domicile as it is used in the Lugano Convention will, therefore, always be defined according to the relevant rules of the PIL.

According to Article 20, para. 1(a), PIL, a natural person is domiciled in the state where the person resides with the intention of staying permanently. The place of residence of a person is the place where the person actually, *i.e.* physically, stays. The further prerequisite for domicile, the intention of staying permanently, has to be determined objectively in the sense that it is not only the subjective internal will of the person which is decisive, but also external elements, such as professional, financial and family ties. On the basis of all these elements, the court has to decide whether the person has made the place of actual settlement the centre of his life in the long term.

Nobody can have more than one domicile. If a person has no domicile, the place of temporary residence is deemed to be his domicile for the purposes of the PIL. The rules of the Swiss Civil Code on domicile and temporary residence are not applicable (Art. 20, para. 2, PIL).

The domicile of a corporate body is its seat (Art. 21, para. 1, PIL). The seat of a corporate body is at the place designated by the bye-laws or the articles of association. If no such place is mentioned in the bye-laws or the articles, then the place of the actual management of the corporate body is considered its domicile (Art. 21, para. 2, PIL).

CHAPTER 8

THE SERVICE OF FOREIGN ORIGINATING PROCESS

8.01. Introduction. It is a requirement of the Conventions that steps should be taken to ensure that a defendant receives any document instituting proceedings against him in sufficient time to enable him to arrange for his defence.

The Conventions recognise the wide currency within the contracting States of the 1965 Hague Convention on the service of Judicial and Extrajudicial Documents in Civil or Commercial Matters[1], by providing that the relevant provisions of that Convention shall apply (as between Member States who are signatories) to the service of proceedings.

The following description of procedures in the various jurisdictions thus largely reflects the scheme of the Hague Convention which effectively caters for three alternative means of service:

(1) through diplomatic channels;
(2) through a designated central authority;
(3) through other means permitted for service of domestic proceedings.

Note
1. Of the signatories to the Brussels Convention only Austria, Iceland and Switzerland are not parties to the Hague Convention.

8.02. England and Wales. There is no objection to service of foreign process within England and Wales either through consular or diplomatic channels or by post. Service will also be effected through the courts when a written request for service is received from the designated central authority (Her Majesty's Principal Secretary of State for Foreign and Commonwealth Affairs) with a recommendation that service be effected; or, where the foreign country concerned is a "Convention Country", from a consular or other authority of that country.

The request must be accompanied by a translation in English, two copies of the process and two copies of a translation thereof. The latter two copies will not be necessary if the foreign court or tribunal certifies that the person to be served understands the language of the process. Service will then be effected by a process server leaving a copy of the process and other documents with the person to be served. The process server sends the Senior Master of the High Court a copy of the process and an affidavit, certificate or report proving due service of process or stating the reason why service could not be effected.

As an alternative to personal service, the process server is authorised to effect service by inserting the process through the letter box of the defendant. The court also has power to authorise substituted service; allowing the court to specify the method of service it deems appropriate.

8.03. Scotland. Service of a foreign process within Scotland may be by one of the competent modes of service, including personal service or service by recorded delivery letter, or by one of the other methods provided by the Hague Convention. These include service through diplomatic or consular agents or through the appropriate central authority in criminal matters. In Scotland the central authority in criminal matters is the Crown Agent.

8.04. Austria. The service of documents of courts and authorities is regulated in the Austrian Act on the Service of Documents of 1982 (Zustellgesetz). Section 12 regulates the service of foreign documents in Austria. According to this section the provisions of any international conventions or bilateral treaties take priority over the rules of the Zustellgesetz. If the foreign authorities require a different procedure from that of Austrian law, such procedure can be implemented if it complies with the principles of Austrian law. The service of a document in a foreign language without a certified German translation is only admissible if the addressee is willing to accept such document. If the addressee does not protest to the authorities who have served the document within three days of service it is assumed that the document has been accepted.

8.05. Belgium. Subject to the provisions of any international conventions, service of foreign originating process within Belgium should be through the intervention of a local bailiff. It cannot be effected by post, by court officials or by local lawyers.

8.06. Denmark. The basis for the service of foreign originating process is the Hague Convention. The documents must state the subject-matter of the case, when and how service is to be effected and the names of the parties to the case. The documents must be in Danish or accompanied by a translation and be provided in duplicate. The documents are submitted to the Danish Ministry of Justice or to the District Courts which will themselves effect service through process servers in accordance with the provisions of the law on civil procedure. The defendant must have time to arrange his defence after service has been effected.

Service of documents may be by post, but it is contingent upon the voluntary participation of the defendant.

8.07. Finland. Finland has ratified the Hague Convention. The central authority designated under the Hague Convention is the Finnish Ministry of Justice and service is effected through the relevant provincial administration. The documents must normally be in Finnish or Swedish or accompanied by a translation.

Service of process can also be effected through a Finnish process server. These are state officials who work in connection with local courts.

8.08. France. The rules governing service of process are to be found either in the Hague Convention or the various bilateral conventions, *e.g.* the French-British Convention of 1934.

For those States party to the Conventions, France will allow the service of foreign originating process through French procedural channels at the direct request of the plaintiff. Otherwise service has to be effected through the central authorities designated under the Hague Convention.

Service at the direct request of the plaintiff will be by a French bailiff. Service by post or through the court is not permitted.

8.09. Germany. Service of foreign process must be through the central authority as required by the Hague Convention. Following a request from their home countries, foreign consular officials may directly request local or district courts to effect service of foreign judicial documents.

Article 7 of the Anglo-German Convention 1928, concerning legal proceedings in civil and commercial matters, allows parties in Great Britain to make a direct request to a bailiff to effect service.

Service by post from abroad and service through a lawyer in Germany is ineffectual.

8.10. Greece. Greece has ratified the Hague Convention. Accordingly service of foreign process can be made as therein provided. Service will be made at the instance of the interested litigant. As yet the provisions for service by post have not become effective. The person may be served wherever he is to be found, unless he has a home, shop, office, laboratory in the place where service is to be effected or works there as a servant or employee. In these cases service may only be effected at the establishments mentioned. Service with the consent of the recipient is always valid, wherever made.

Service of process must be to the addressee or, for legal persons, to their lawful representative. If the person to be served is not at home, valid service can be effected upon any of his co-habitants.

8.11. Ireland. Ireland has ratified the Hague Convention. The service of foreign proceedings may therefore be made as provided therein.

8.12. Italy. Unless bilateral or international conventions are applicable, service of process is governed by the rules of the Code of Civil Procedure. Service of foreign originating process requires the special authorisation of the public prosecutor at the Tribunal with jurisdiction over the place where notice is to be given. In order to obtain such authorisation, the party who intends to serve foreign process in Italy sends a certified copy of the original document to the relevant court official together with as many copies thereof as there are persons to whom the act must be notified. The certified copy must be accompanied by a translation and a certificate from the Italian lawyer who has been appointed. The court official submits the document to the competent public prosecutor who will decide whether to authorise service. There can be no appeal from his decision. Once authorisation is obtained, the court official will effect service in compliance with the applicable rules.

Service can also be requested through diplomatic channels, in which case a consular or diplomatic agent will apply directly to the public prosecutor for authority to serve process.

8.13. Luxembourg. Service is generally effected through the central authority designated in accordance with the provisions of the Hague Convention.

8.14. The Netherlands. Service of foreign originating process may be through the central authority nominated in accordance with the Hague Convention, namely the public prosecutor with the district court of the Hague. In that instance the central authority will forward the document to the public prosecutor for the district court where the defendant has his residence. The public prosecutor sends the document to the Deurwaarder who will serve it on the addressee. Alternatively, and more frequently, the competent public prosecutor sends the document to the police who serve the document. The document is then sent back to the public prosecutor who completes the certificate and sends both to the central authority.

The Netherlands have not objected to the transmission of foreign originating process either through the consular, or diplomatic channels, postal channels, or through the Deurwaarder. In addition the Netherlands have declared that the public prosecutor of a District Court other than the central authority may receive and take action on requests for service under Articles 3 to 6 of the Hague Convention.

8.15. Norway. Under the Hague Convention foreign originating process may be submitted for service to the Norwegian Ministry of Justice as the designated central authority, alternatively, under the Convention, documents may also be sent directly to the relevant local court through the appropriate diplomatic channels. In addition, under the terms of separate multi-/bilateral agreements, documents originating from Sweden, Denmark, Finland, Iceland or Germany may be sent directly to the relevant local court by the competent authorities in the country of origin.

Service of the documents in question will then be implemented by the local court having jurisdiction over the area in which the individual on whom the documents are to be served is domiciled. If the documents are not in Norwegian, Swedish or Danish, they must normally be accompanied by a translation into such language. Service will normally take place in accordance with the procedures applicable to the service of a petition or writ issued under Norwegian law.

8.16. Portugal. Portugal has approved the Hague Convention. This does not however prevent the service of process through the post or through the Portuguese courts.

8.17. Spain. Spanish legal authorities will assist in the service of foreign process pursuant to the provisions of international agreements and treaties to which Spain is a signatory, and in their absence, depending on the existence of reciprocity of treatment.

Spain is a signatory to certain multilateral international treaties and has subscribed to other bilateral treaties covering different aspects of international judicial co-operation. The most important of the former is the treaty of The Hague, July 17, 1905, which was replaced by the Treaty of March 1, 1954 ratified by Spain on April 12, 1957. Spain is also party to the Hague Convention 1965.

Reciprocity of treatment must be verified or offered by the requesting foreign legal authority. Confirmation of reciprocity with the requesting State will be given by the Spanish Government through the Ministry of Justice.

If the above criteria are fulfilled, assistance can only be refused in the following circumstances:

(1) when the process for which the application is made concerns a matter within the exclusive jurisdiction of the Spanish courts;
(2) when the act requested is not within the powers of the recipient authority from which it is requested. In this case, the latter will refer the request to the competent authority;
(3) when the request does not comply with the requirements for verifying its authenticity or is not made in the Spanish language;
(4) when the co-operation requested is contrary to public order.

The legal steps to be taken in Spain which are requested by foreign courts are entrusted to those bodies as provided in the relevant international treaties. In the absence of such provision, the matter is dealt with by the Ministry of Justice, the request being addressed through the Ministry of Foreign Affairs.

8.18. Sweden. A decree (1909:24 s.1), based on the Hague Convention of 1905, provides that foreign authorities can send requests for service in Sweden to the Department of Foreign Affairs. The Department will normally ensure that the request for service is effected. If the documents are not in either Swedish, Norwegian or Danish, or accompanied by a certified translation into any of those languages, the intended recipient may refuse to accept service.

Documents originating in Denmark, Finland, Iceland or Norway may be sent for service directly to the competent local authority in Sweden. Service will usually be effected in accordance with the procedures provided for under Swedish law.

8.19. Switzerland. Service of judicial documents is considered an official act in Switzerland and may not be carried out by private individuals directly.

Service of foreign originating process is carried out within the framework of legal assistance provided by the Swiss authorities. Switzerland is a signatory to the 1905 and 1954 Hague Conventions on Civil Procedure. In 1994, Switzerland also ratified the 1965 Hague Convention on the Service Abroad of Judicial and Extrajudicial Documents which entered into force on January 1, 1995. The Convention provides for a system of central authorities through which service takes place. In Switzerland the cantons are assigned the task of establishing the central authority in the sense of Article 2 of the Convention. As this leads to 26 different central authorities and because it might be difficult for a foreign judicial authority to determine which of these 26 central authorities is competent, the request may alternatively be addressed to the Federal Office for Police Matters (OPM) which will forward it to the competent cantonal central authority without prior examination. In the Canton of Zurich the Cantonal High Court is the central authority according to Article 2 of the Convention.

Switzerland has made reservations against the procedures provided for by Articles 8 and 10 of the Convention, thereby excluding the direct service of documents between foreign and Swiss judicial authorities or between foreign authorities and private individuals staying in Switzerland. The direct service of foreign originating process by post to a Swiss resident is, as a consequence, still excluded. An exception is only made for service by diplomatic or consular representatives of a foreign state in Switzerland to nationals of that foreign state provided they accept service without coercion.

Switzerland has also deposited a reservation against the direct way of communication provided for by Article IV of the protocol no. 1 to the Lugano Convention.

Concerning the service of judicial documents there exist bilateral treaties with various countries (Belgium, Germany, Austria, France, Italy, Luxembourg, Poland and Hungary) which provide for direct ways of communication between the competent courts, or between central authorities.

Where no direct way of communication (between courts or central authorities) is granted by treaty, letters of request have to be sent through diplomatic channels to the OPM which will examine them and determine whether they meet the standards and requirements of the relevant Conventions. Requests of countries which are not signatories to the 1905 and 1954 Hague Conventions are customarily treated on the basis of comity and reciprocity within the framework of these Conventions. The request will then be forwarded to a central cantonal authority for the canton concerned which will then remit the request to the locally competent judicial authority. For service of foreign originating process this will be a judge or court at the domicile of the defendant. The competent authority will then effect service on the defendant personally or to an adult family member living in the same household by post against special acknowledgement of receipt. If this is not possible, service may also be effected by the bailiff or police.

CHAPTER 9

SECURITY FOR COSTS

9.01. Introduction. One hazard of international litigation has always been the vulnerability of foreign plaintiffs to being required in many jurisdictions to post security for the legal costs to be reimbursed to the defendant in the event of an unsuccessful claim. The Conventions recognise this hazard to the extent of forbidding any requirement that security be given in proceedings to register a judgment from another contracting State.

In general, the fact that the judgments and orders will now be readily recognised throughout the contracting States means that the need for security should be less obvious and the willingness to award security in a European context ought accordingly to decline. As will appear, however, the position is far from uniform ranging from quite sweeping provisions for security in Spain to Italy and Portugal where no provision for security exists at all.

9.02. England and Wales. In the High Court a plaintiff will have to provide security for costs, when it appears to the court:

(1) (a) that the plaintiff is ordinarily resident out of the jurisdiction; or
 (b) the plaintiff is a nominal plaintiff suing for the benefit of someone else and there is reason to think that the plaintiff will be unable to pay the costs of the defendant, if requested to do so; or
 (c) the plaintiff's address is not stated in the writ or is incorrectly stated therein; or
 (d) the plaintiff has changed his address during the course of the proceedings with a view to evading the consequences of litigation; and
(2) in the circumstances of the case the court considers it just.

In addition where the plaintiff to an action is a limited company, the court may order security to be given for costs if it appears that the plaintiff will be unable to pay the defendant's costs if the defendant is successful in its defence.

The above criteria apply whether the plaintiff is foreign or a national of England and Wales. Thus, the courts will not discriminate against a foreign national on the basis of nationality. Residence abroad is also not a ground for ordering the plaintiff to give security, it is a pre-condition. As in all the other circumstances, the court has a discretion whether to order security for costs to be given by a plaintiff resident abroad. In deciding whether to order security, the court will take into account the plaintiff's prospects of success, admissions by the defendant, open offers and payments into court.

Generally security will not be ordered from a plaintiff resident abroad if there is a co-plaintiff resident in the jurisdiction or if the plaintiff has substantial real or personal property in England or Wales.

A County Court judge has power to order security for costs on similar principles to those outlined above, when it appears that the plaintiff is ordinarily resident outside England and Wales.

9.03. Scotland. Whether to order security for expenses is always a matter for the court's discretion. The courts have power to order a pursuer who is resident abroad to sist a mandatory (*i.e.* nominate a person within the Scottish jurisdiction) who will take personal responsibility for the expenses and day-to-day conduct of the case. Each case is special to its own facts but an important consideration against making such an order is that there exists an effective system for enforcing any Scottish Decree in the pursuer's own country. As in England, where the pursuer is a limited company, the court may order security to be found if the company appears to be unable to pay the defender's expenses.

9.04. Austria. When foreign nationals appear before an Austrian court as plaintiff they are obliged to provide security for the costs of the proceedings if security is requested by the defendant. This rule is subject to any contrary provision in international conventions to which Austria is party.

A plaintiff will not have to provide security:

(1) if he has his usual residence in Austria;
(2) if a court decision that the plaintiff shall reimburse the costs of the proceedings to the defendant would be enforceable in the country where the plaintiff has his usual residence;

(3) if the plaintiff possesses sufficient assets within the jurisdiction to cover the costs of the proceedings;
(4) in actions regarding marital disputes, mandates and bills of exchange;
(5) where the plaintiff is a counterclaimant;
(6) for actions brought by public summons (Infolge öffentlicher gerichtlicher Aufforderung).

Security for costs must be requested during the preliminary court hearing and before the main proceedings begin.

9.05. Belgium. Plaintiffs who are foreign nationals have to pay security for costs where it is requested by a Belgian defendant. This rule is, however, subject to the provisions of any international treaties. Security will therefore not be demanded of plaintiffs who are nationals of contracting States.

9.06. Denmark. Should the defendant so request, a foreign plaintiff must provide security for costs, unless Danish nationals are exempted from paying such security in the state of the foreign plaintiff.

9.07. Finland. There are no provisions requiring foreign plaintiffs to provide security for costs in Finland.

9.08. France. The obligation to pay costs is limited in any event in France. Under no circumstances will a foreign plaintiff be obliged to provide security for costs in proceedings before the French court.

9.09. Germany. Under the provisions of the German Law on Civil Procedure a national sued by a non-national has a right to demand security for legal costs. However, under the same rules a number of special proceedings are excluded from this general rule: summary proceedings on documents alone; counterclaims and suits in connection with registered title in land. Further restrictions are imposed by international treaties. A consequence of these restrictions is that the right to security for costs only exists against plaintiffs from about 20 countries in the world which are, without exception, developing countries.

9.10. Greece. There are no special rules requiring foreign plaintiffs to provide security for costs. A defendant has the right to petition for security for costs against a plaintiff where he can show that there is an obvious risk that he will not be able to enforce any award of costs to him.

9.11. Ireland. The Rules of the Superior Courts provide that in certain circumstances a foreign plaintiff may be required to give security for costs. However, in all applications for security for costs, the defendant must file an affidavit to show that he has a defence to the plaintiff's claim on the merits. This affidavit must be sworn by the defendant; it is not sufficient for it to be sworn by the defendant's solicitor. Although the courts have wide discretion whether to order security for costs, a defendant has a prima facie entitlement to security where the plaintiff resides outside the jurisdiction. Having said this, the courts have displayed increasing reluctance to order security for costs.

The measure, time and form of the security will be determined by the Master of the High Court. As a general rule security will be ordered for about one third of the costs likely to be incurred by the defendant.

Security for costs may not be demanded of a foreign plaintiff in proceedings for the enforcement of a judgment under the Conventions solely on the basis that the plaintiff is a foreign national or that he is not domiciled or resident in Ireland. It is still uncertain whether security can be demanded from a foreign plaintiff domiciled in another contracting State in other proceedings. However, it would seem likely that the Irish courts will follow the decisions in the English courts.

9.12. Italy. There is no right to demand security for costs in legal proceedings irrespective of whether the plaintiff is Italian or foreign.

9.13. Luxembourg. There is a right under the Luxembourg Code of Civil Procedure which allows a defendant to demand security for costs from a foreign plaintiff. However, due to the extent that the obligation to provide security has been abolished by international convention, such security will not be requested in practice.

9.14. The Netherlands. Subject to the terms of international conventions, a foreign plaintiff will normally be ordered to pay security for costs on the application of the defendant. The amount will be fixed by the court based on its estimate of the possible cost of the proceedings. Security can take any suitable form, for example a bank guarantee. A foreign plaintiff with immoveable assets in the Netherlands may submit to a charge on those assets as security.

9.15. Norway. The Norwegian Civil Procedure Act 1915 grants the defendant a right to demand that a foreign plaintiff provide security for the defendant's costs of defence. The level of security is fixed by the court presiding over the case, and should reflect the level of costs likely to be awarded to the defendant in the event that judgment should be given in favour of the defendant.

However, in most cases the right to security for costs from a foreign plaintiff has been abolished under one of the number of international conventions ratified by Norway which abolish the right to demand security for costs from litigants whose countries are party to the Conventions.

9.16. Portugal. There is no provision under Portuguese law requiring a foreign plaintiff to provide security for costs.

9.17. Spain. The Spanish Law on Civil Procedure imposes an obligation on foreign claimants to guarantee payment of costs of the process in the event that their claim is dismissed. In most cases this requirement is not enforced due to the various international treaties accepted by almost all countries in the world which abolish the right to security from a foreign litigant; for example, the Hague Convention of October 25, 1980. In the event of there being no applicable treaty, Spanish law will apply the principle of reciprocity. It is then for the defendant alleging that security is necessary to prove that security for costs would be required from Spanish claimants in the claimant's country.

The law requires the deposit of certain security for the filing of appeals by way of re-hearing and on a point of law. This requirement was imposed by the legislature in order to avoid the filing of appeals intended exclusively to delay enforcement of judgments. Security is only required for appeals by way of rehearing when the first and second instance judgments are both against the appellant. This security consists of a deposit of 50,000.00 pesetas regardless of the nationality of the appellant.

9.18. Sweden. An act (SFS 1980:307) entitles a defendant to demand that a foreign plaintiff provides security for the defendant's costs that the plaintiff may be ordered to pay. The security must be provided by way of a direct payment undertaking on the part of a guarantor. Should the defendant not approve the security, its sufficiency will be tried by the court. Forms of security other than a direct payment undertaking may be provided with the defendant's consent.

The defendant must make the request for security when he makes his first submissions in the case.

In so far as Sweden has agreed in international conventions certain foreign citizens or foreign legal persons are not obliged to provide such security. Sweden has acceded *inter alia* to the Hague Conventions of July 17, 1905 and March 1, 1954. Citizens domiciled in countries which are parties to these Conventions accordingly do not need to provide security for litigation costs.

9.19. Switzerland. Whether a foreign plaintiff has to post security for legal costs depends on the applicable cantonal Civil Procedure Code.

In the Canton of Zurich a foreign plaintiff without domicile in Switzerland can be obliged to post security for legal costs, unless an international treaty provides otherwise. In this connection it is the Hague Convention on Civil Procedure of July 17, 1905, as amended on March 1, 1954, to which Switzerland is a signatory, which is relevant. All the nationals of a signatory state with domicile in a signatory state are exempted from the obligation to post security. There are also a number of bilateral treaties to the same effect.

In 1994 Switzerland has also ratified the 1980 Hague Convention on the International Access to the Judiciary. The Convention entered into force on January 1, 1995. All natural persons and corporate bodies with residence in a signatory state will be exempted from the obligation to post security for legal costs.

The Civil Procedure Code for the Canton of Zurich lists other grounds on which a plaintiff may be required to post security for costs and which are not subject to the exemptions in the Hague Conventions. They are all grounds which deal with the potentially weak financial situation of the plaintiff.

Security for costs cannot be imposed in certain proceedings, such as litigation in connection with an employment contract.

The amount of security to be posted is established on the basis of the value of the claim as well as on the prospective difficulty and length of the proceedings. If the requisite security is not put up within the time-limit set by the court, the action will be dismissed on that ground.

Court orders on security for costs are subject to appeal.

CHAPTER 10

THE RECOGNITION AND ENFORCEMENT OF JUDGMENTS THROUGHOUT THE CONTRACTING STATES TO THE BRUSSELS CONVENTION AND THE LUGANO CONVENTION

10.01. Introduction. The end product of the Conventions' regime is, in effect, a passport which enables a judgment of any contracting State to be converted into a judgment of any other contracting State. The nature of the objective is to turn what could otherwise be a judicial exercise into an administrative one.

It appears that the Conventions have succeeded in this objective to the extent that all the contracting States have a system which is superficially very similar in all respects. This flows naturally from the common rules of procedure set down in the Conventions which we describe before turning to their application in individual contracting States.

Article 26 lays down the basic principle that recognition of a judgment of a court of another contracting State should not require a special procedure. Further, if a question of recognition arises which is incidental to a matter already before a court, that court shall have jurisdiction over the question. Recognition should only be refused on the grounds of Articles 27 and 28. The question of public policy under Article 27(1) is dealt with further below. However it is sacrosanct that a judgment may not be reviewed on its merits; Article 29.

If a judgment has been appealed in its State of origin, this is a ground upon which enforcement or recognition proceedings may be stayed.

Article 32 sets out the courts to which applications for enforcement are to be submitted. Local jurisdiction within the contracting State is determined by the domicile of the party against whom enforcement is sought, or, if he is a non-domiciliary, by reference to the place of enforcement.

The procedure for making an application is governed by the law of the State where enforcement is sought. An applicant must give an address for service within the area of jurisdiction of the competent court. Alternatively, where, under national procedure, no provision exists for the giving of such an address, the applicant must appoint a representative *ad litem*.

Applications are to be initially *ex parte* and may be refused only on the grounds set out in Articles 27 and 28. The provisions of Article 28 in the Lugano Convention provide for slightly wider grounds for the refusal of the recognition of a judgment than the Brussels Convention. The court's decision must be made without delay.

A defendant has one month from service to appeal a decision authorising enforcement. This time period will be extended to two months when the defendant is not domiciled in the contracting State where enforcement is sought. There can be no extension of time on account of distance.

Articles 37 and 40 set out the courts to whom appeals against authorisation and refusal are to be made. If appeal has been lodged against judgment in the State where judgment was given, or the time for appeal has not yet expired, the court may stay the proceedings and in the latter instance specify the time within which appeal is to be lodged. The court also has the power to make enforcement conditional on the provision of security.

When hearing the application for enforcement, the court may also consider the grant of any protective measures sought by the applicant. During the time for appeal and determination thereof no steps may be taken to enforce the judgment other than protective measures.

Articles 46 and 47 of the Convention set out the documents required to accompany any application. If the applicant fails to produce the required documents, the court may specify a time for their production, accept equivalent documents or, if it considers that it has sufficient information before it, dispense with their production. The court may require translations of any documents certified by persons entitled to do so in one of the Contracting States.

10.02. England and Wales. English courts do not issue a specific order authorising enforcement of a foreign judgment, rather enforcement is by means of registration of the judgment with the appropriate court, usually the High Court. Registration gives the judgment the same force and effect as if it were a judgment of that court.

The application for registration is made by an interested party to a Master of the Queen's Bench Division. However, if the registration is in respect of an injunction or for the grant of a receiver, then the application must be made to a judge. This avenue should also be used when the application for registration is linked with a request for protective measures which under English law are the exclusive preserve of a judge. This would encompass Mareva Injunctions and Anton Piller Orders. As with all *ex parte* hearings, the applicant bears a duty of full and frank disclosure.

The application must be supported by an affidavit exhibiting the documents required under Articles 46 and 47 of the Convention. This includes certified translations if the documents are not already in English. The affidavit must give an address within the jurisdiction for service of the process on the applicant and state, in so far as it is known, the name and the usual or last known address or place of business of the person against whom judgment is sought. The affidavit must state the grounds upon which the applicant is entitled to enforce the judgment and that, at the date of the application, the judgment is unsatisfied or the extent to which the judgment is unsatisfied.

The order for registration will be drawn up by the applicant. Notification of the decision to the applicant will usually be made in person by the Master at the hearing

The defendant will be notified of the decision by the applicant. Until notice has been served, the time for appeal does not start to run. The formalities of service follow those for the service of writs, although no leave is required for service out of the jurisdiction. Enforcement will be stayed pending the expiry of the time for appeal, although the applicant can invoke any protective measures.

An appeal against a decision to refuse registration is made by summons *inter partes* to the Judge in Chambers. Pursuant to the Rules of the Supreme Court, Order 71, rule 33(2)(b), the time limit for appeal is one month from the date of refusal.

An appeal by the defendant is also by *inter partes* summons to the Judge in Chambers. The time limits are those set out in Articles 39 of the Conventions. Institution of an appeal stays enforcement until the appeal has been heard. Under the Rules of the Supreme Court the court has power to extend the time for appeal if an application for such extension is made by a defendant not domiciled within the jurisdiction within the two month time limit for appeal. There must be some question whether the exercise of this discretion to extend the time limits is compatible with the Conventions.

Appeal from the Judge in Chambers is to the Court of Appeal. Further appeal will lie on a point of law to the House of Lords.

Public policy objections may possibly be taken under Article 27(1) in the event of fraud or breach of natural justice in the original proceedings leading to judgment. The issue of fraud cannot, however, be raised if it has been argued before the court at trial as this would be a review of the judgment on its merits.

10.03. Scotland. The procedure for recognition and enforcement of non-Scottish judgments depends on the country where the judgments were originally given.

10.03:1. Contracting States under the Conventions. Provided the judgment is within the scope of these Conventions the procedure is as follows:

An application, accompanied by specified documents, is made to the Court of Session. It is normally considered without any need for appearance by the applicant. If the Court is satisfied that all requirements have been complied with and that recognition is not contrary to Articles 27 or 28 of the relevant Convention, it grants a warrant for registration of the judgment and grants decree either in terms of the original judgment, or, if necessary, in accordance with Scots law.

A certified copy of the Court of Session's order and a certified copy of the judgment to be registered (together with a certified translation, if not in English) is registered in the Books of Council and Session. An extract (official copy) of the registered judgment with warrant for execution is issued to the applicant.

The applicant intimates to the person against whom judgment was given and against whom enforcement is sought. Prior to intimation, the applicant may apply for protective measures (see Chapter 5) against the property of the person against whom judgment was obtained, as long as intimation is made within 21 days of such protective measures.

There is a provision for appeal, both by an applicant against refusal of registration and by a person against whom judgment was granted against the authorisation of enforcement measures.

10.03:2. England and Wales; Northern Ireland.

(1) *Money Judgments.* The applicant obtains a certificate in a prescribed form from the original court. This is registered in the Books of Counsel and Session. An extract is issued to the applicant with warrant for execution. The applicant may proceed to enforce the judgment and do diligence on that extract.

(2) *Non-Money Judgments.* The applicant makes an application in a prescribed form and accompanied by specified documents to the Court of Session. The application is usually considered without appearance by the applicant. If satisfied, the Court grants decree in accordance with Scots law. A certified copy of the judgment is then registered in the Register of the Books of Council and Session. The applicant is issued with an extract of the registered judgment with warrant for execution. The applicant may proceed to enforce the judgment and do diligence on that extract.

10.03:3. Judgments of Courts of Countries which are not party to the Conventions and Judgments otherwise outside the scope of the Conventions.

There is a miscellany of other enactments providing for registration of a foreign judgment in the books of Scottish courts and its subsequent enforcement as though it were a Scottish judgment. In addition, the Scottish courts may recognise foreign decrees at common law as long as the foreign court had jurisdiction at the time the proceedings were initiated, the action was not a penal or revenue action, the foreign court conducted the proceedings in a judicial manner and was not misled by any party's fraud and the judgment obtained is final. The party seeking to enforce a foreign decree which is not enforceable under a statutory regime must first raise an action in the Court of Session for a decree-conform founding on the foreign decree itself. If the Court recognises the foreign decree, applying the principles set out above, it grants decree in conformity with it, with warrant for execution on the Scottish decree.

Where a foreign decree may be enforced under the 1982 Act, the court has no competence to enforce it by "decree-conform".

10.04. Austria. The Brussels and the Lugano Conventions have not as yet been ratified in Austria.

Foreign judgments will be enforced on the basis of deeds and legal instruments issued abroad as long as they are enforceable according to the laws of the corresponding country of origin and subject either to the express provision of Austrian law or the degree to which reciprocity of enforcement exists under the numerous multi- and bilateral treaties to which Austria is party.

Further preconditions for the enforcement of a judgment in Austria are:

(1) that the action was brought on the basis of laws valid in the country where judgment was given;
(2) that the foreign originating process which began the proceedings before the foreign court or foreign authority have been properly served, either in that country, Austria, or another state;
(3) that the judgment is confirmed as being enforceable by the foreign court or other competent authority.

Grounds on which the enforcement of a judgment might be refused include that the enforcement required according to the laws of the country of origin is either not possible or is illegal under Austrian law or would constitute a breach of Austrian public order.

Application for a certificate of enforceability must be made in writing or orally to the regional court with jurisdiction over the area where the person against whom enforcement is sought has his legal domicile. If such a domicile does not exist, the application must be made to the regional court with jurisdiction over the area where enforcement is to take place.

The person against whom enforcement is sought has an initial right to appeal the enforcement to the court granting enforcement or, if such a party has not been granted the right to file a statement, to the appellate court within 14 days of notice of enforcement. In certain circumstances, there is a further right of appeal to the Supreme Court of Justice.

10.05. Belgium. Application for the enforcement of a judgment is made to the Court of First Instance (Tribunal de Première Instance). The relevant documents as set out in Articles 46 and 47 must accompany the petition and must be supported by certified translations in the language of the petition.

The decision of the court as to enforcement will be notified to the applicant by mail. The applicant must then have the decision served upon the defendant by a bailiff. If the defendant wishes to appeal the decision on enforcement he must apply through the so-called "opposition" procedure to the Court of First Instance. The procedure is initiated by the service of a writ of summons by a bailiff.

An applicant who has been refused the enforcement of his judgment, must turn to the Court of Appeal (Cour d'Appel). The appeal can be initiated either by writ of summons served by a bailiff or by the filing of a request with the Greffe (Clerks Office) of the Court of Appeal.

Further appeal against decisions refusing or authorising enforcement is only by way of review on the law to the Supreme Court (Cour de Cassation/Hof van Cassatie). The appeal must be begun by petition to the Greffe of that Court lodged by an Avocat à la Cour de Cassation (a member of the Bar to the Supreme Court). There are eighteen such avocats within Belgium.

Belgium has not so far invoked Article 27 and refused recognition or enforcement of any judgment on the grounds of public policy. The most recent case of refusal of enforcement on public policy grounds was outside the scope of the Conventions. The court refused to enforce a judgment allowing a husband to divorce his Moroccan wife without her consent.

10.06. Denmark. Application for the enforcement of a judgment is made to the Sheriff's Court (Fogedret) within the jurisdiction of the local court of the defendant's domicile. If the defendant is not domiciled in Denmark, the application for enforcement is filed with the Sheriff's Court which is competent under the general provisions of civil procedure; Article 487 of the Law on Civil Procedure. The application is accompanied by the documents as set out in Articles 46 and 47. The relevant Sheriff's Court can require certified translations and the person seeking enforcement must specify a party in Denmark for communications regarding the case.

The application for enforcement is made *ex parte* and enforcement can only be refused on the grounds set out in Articles 27 and 28 of the Convention. There are no public policy restrictions on enforcement or recognition. The court does have power to consider whether the judgment concerns matters properly the subject of the Convention within Article 1 thereof.

Notification of the decision of the Sheriff's Court is to the creditor or his representative. If the decision authorises enforcement, the Sheriff's Court will serve the decision on the defendant.

Appeal against a decision authorising enforcement is to the High Court having jurisdiction over the pertinent City Court. Under Article 10 of the Convention, the appeal against enforcement may be stayed if the judgment in question has been appealed.

Further appeal to the Supreme Court from the decision of the High Court requires leave from the Ministry of Justice: Articles 371 and 392 of the Law on Civil Procedure.

10.07. Finland. Application for the enforcement of a judgment is made to the District Court (käräjäoikeus) for the area in which the defendant is domiciled. If the defendant is not domiciled in Finland at all, application is made to the District Court for the area where enforcement will take place. Applications may also be sent to the Finnish Ministry of Justice which will forward the application to the competent District Court. The relevant documents as set out in Articles 46 and 47 of the Lugano Convention must accompany the application and must normally be supported by translations.

The decision of the court regarding enforcement will be given in the office of the relevant court. It can also be sent to the applicant by post. The applicant must then have the decision served upon the defendant by a bailiff.

Appeal against a decision authorising enforcement is to the Court of Appeal in whose jurisdiction the relevant district court is situated. Further appeal is to the Supreme Court.

10.08. France. The initial application for the enforcement of a judgment is made by petition (requête) to the President of the First Instance Civil Court (Tribunal de Grande Instance). The petition must be filed by an avocat and be accompanied by the documents set out in Articles 46 and 47 of the Conventions. There is no need to serve translations of the documents with the petition.

The competent first instance civil court is either that of the defendant's domicile or, if he is not domiciled in France, the court for the area where the defendant has assets. The President of the Court must confirm of his own motion that he has territorial jurisdiction.

Notification of the decision authorising enforcement has no special form. The decision is communicated to the avocat of the applicant by the Clerk of the Court.

Appeal against a decision authorising enforcement is begun by lodging a statement (opposition) with the Court of Appeal (Cour d'Appel) within one month of service of the decision (Ordonnance sur Requête).

Appeal against refusal of enforcement is again to the Court of Appeal. A déclaration d'appel must be filed with the Clerk of the Court. Although no time limit for lodging the appeal is set down in either the Conventions or the Nouveau Code de Procédure Civile (NCPC; New Code of Procedure), there is some authority that one should observe the 15-day time limit set down by Article 496, NCPC, for appeal from Ordonnances sur Requête. The 15-day period runs from notification to the applicant himself and not to his avocat.

In both cases, opposition and déclaration d'appel, judgment is given by the Court of Appeal after an *inter partes* hearing

Appeal from the order of the Court of Appeal is to the Court of Cassation by a statement lodged at the Clerks' Office for the Court of Cassation. The statement must be filed by an avocat admitted to that Court (Avocat aux Conseils) within two months and all pleadings must be completed within five months of filing.

There are no significant public policy requirements in France which would prevent the recognition or enforcement of a judgment within the Conventions. However, in considering the issue of public policy in general the French courts distinguish between rights created in France and those arising outside of France. The former must comply with the entire scope of French public policy. The latter may still be recognised even if they contradict certain elements of French public policy. There is a proviso to this so-called Effet Atténué de l'Ordre Public. It will not apply if the foreign decision is perceived as being particularly inequitable and the situation is closely linked to France.

10.09. **Germany.** The procedure for recognition substantially follows the procedure for the issue of a Certificate of Enforceability: Article 27, AVAG. Proceedings for such a certificate are begun by an application to the presiding judge of a civil chamber of the Regional Court (Landgericht) with jurisdiction over the area where the defendant has his residence. If the defendant has no residence within Germany, then jurisdiction lies with the court for the district where the enforcement measures are to be pursued. Usually this is the district where the defendant's assets are located. Under the AVAG the respective Regional Court has exclusive jurisdiction. Consequently any jurisdiction agreement between the parties regarding matters of enforcement will not be regarded as enforceable.

The application for a Certificate of Enforceability can be made either orally or in writing for the record of the appropriate court office. The documents required by the German courts to accompany such an application follow the provisions of Articles 46 and 47. In addition the court may demand certified translations of the documents. An applicant must also designate a person authorised to accept service who is domiciled within the court's district. Pending the appointment of such a person, the documents may be served by mail. The hearing itself will generally be *ex parte* and on the documents alone. If the court grants a Certificate of Enforceability, an execution clause is attached to the judgment. Certified copies of the judgment and, if necessary, the translations will then be served on the debtor. The originals are returned to the applicant.

Appeal against a decision on the issue of a Certificate of Enforceability is to the Court of Appeal (Oberlandesgericht). Appeal must be lodged within one month of service of the decision. Although appeal is only to the Court of Appeal, time will also cease to run if the notice of appeal is filed with the Regional Court instead of the Court of Appeal.

Further appeal is restricted to points of law only and goes to the Federal Court of Justice (Bundesgerichtshof). Again there is a time limit of one month from service of the order of the Court of Appeal within which to file the notice of appeal. Grounds of appeal must be filed within one month thereafter.

German courts will examine the question of the compatibility of the enforcement or recognition of a foreign judgment with public policy from both a procedural and a substantive point of view. From the procedural aspect, recognition will be refused if the court considers that the judgment was given following proceedings that failed to meet the concept of due process in German procedural law.

German jurisprudence also ascribes a non-exhaustive character to Article 27(4). Thus, the courts will rely not only on Article 27(4) but also Article 27(1) to examine substantively whether the recognition of a foreign judgment is inconsistent with the basic principles of international private law underpinning German law and its concept of justice. Examples of this doctrine in practice include the view that foreign judgments wrongly failing to apply German anti-trust law to a competitive restraint with implications in Germany cannot be recognised. The test applied by the courts in these cases looks to whether the specific application of foreign law is so inconsistent with national law as to be untenable.

10.10. Greece. There is a presumption in favour of the enforcement of foreign judgments and other instruments of title. Judgments outside the Conventions will be recognised if they satisfy the following criteria:

(1) the issuing court had jurisdiction over the case under the provisions of Greek procedural law;
(2) the defeated litigant was not deprived of a right of defence and of participation in the trial generally, (unless this was pursuant to a provision applicable without discrimination to citizens and non-citizens of the State of the issuing court);
(3) the judgment does not infringe a decision by a Greek court issued on the same matter and acting as *res judicata* against the parties affected by the foreign judgment;
(4) the judgment does not infringe the principle of public policy.

Under Greek law a foreign judgment will be deemed to infringe public policy where it brings about results or creates a situation within Greece which is incompatible with the moral, ethical, legal, political, social and economic order on which regulation is founded.

The court which has jurisdiction to issue an order for the enforcement of a foreign judgment or other instrument of title is the single-member Court of First Instance for the area of domicile, or else of the habitual residence, of the debtor, otherwise the Athens single-member Court of First Instance. The procedure is one of voluntary jurisdiction.

Judgments issued by a contracting State to the Convention will be enforceable provided they are properly issued in their State of origin and otherwise comply with the requirements of Articles 27 to 29 of the relevant Convention. The competent court is, in the first place, the single-member Court with jurisdiction over the defendant's place of domicile or, otherwise, over the place of enforcement. The possibility of jurisdiction being exercised by the court with jurisdiction over the place of enforcement represents an extension of Greek law by the Conventions.

There is some doubt as to the procedure to be followed for the enforcement of a foreign judgment. For non-Convention judgments, it is a matter of voluntary jurisdiction, however the provisions of Articles 46 and 47 of the Convention more closely resemble the procedure for the issue of a Payment Order.

The practice mostly followed by the courts and the lawyers is for an order for enforcement to be issued on submitting a petition *ex parte* to the single-member Court of the place of domicile of the debtor. Under this procedure and contrary to Articles 46 and 47 the necessary supporting documents are not served with the petition, but with the written submissions. The supporting documentation is a certified copy of the judgment, evidence of service in a manner valid under the State of the judgment to be enforced and evidence that the judgment is enforceable in the State of its origin. Evidence of the validity of service and enforceability of the judgment is provided by a legal opinion from a lawyer of the State of origin. All documents are served duly translated into Greek, and the court will reserve judgment (which may delay the matter about a month). A copy of the court's decision will then be served upon the person against whom enforcement proceedings are to be taken and the usual enforcement procedure follows.

For cases outside the Conventions, the defendant is entitled to bring an appeal against the judgment of the court ordering enforcement. The appeal is before the Court of Appeal for the single-member Court issuing the decision ordering enforcement. For cases under the Convention, the remedy available is not called Efesis (appeal) but Prosphygi (recourse). This is, however, brought before the Court of Appeal under Articles 37 and 40 of the relevant Convention.

Since, in this instance, Prosphygi is not technically an appeal, it is submitted that proceedings should be begun pursuant to the provisions of Greek procedural law for the commencement of an action and not for the filing of an appeal. In other words it is not enough solely to file the appeal, one must serve it as well.

In contrast an appeal by the petitioner for the order of enforcement is clearly an "appeal" and should be treated as such. No time period for the filing of the appeal is set down in the Convention and consequently domestic provisions apply. At this stage, the defendant should be summoned by the appellant by service of the appeal on him.

Either party may appeal the decision of the Court of Appeal by filing an appeal in the second degree (Anairesis) with the Areios Pagos.

10.11. Ireland. Any application for the recognition or enforcement of a judgment is made to the Master of the High Court. This application is made *ex parte* and on affidavit evidence. Strict compliance with the provisions of the Conventions, the

Jurisdiction of Courts and Enforcement of Judgments (European Communities) Act 1988 and the Rules of the Superior Courts (No. 1) 1989 is essential. The documents in support, as listed in Articles 46 and 47, must be exhibited to the affidavit. The affidavit must also state whether the judgment provides for the payment of a sum or sums of money; whether interest is recoverable on the judgment and for what period and at what rate. In addition it should contain an address within Ireland for service of the proceedings and, to the best of the deponent's knowledge and belief, the name and usual or last known address or place of business of the person against whom judgment is given. In relation to the judgment itself, the affidavit must contain the grounds upon which the right to enforce is vested in the person making the application and a statement that at the date of the application the judgment has not been wholly or partly satisfied. Practically, the difficulty is usually to convince the Master that the proceedings have been properly served upon the respondent.

Where the documents required by the Rules of Court are not produced, the Master may adjourn the application to allow an opportunity to produce the documents or, alternatively, accept equivalent documents or dispense with the production of documents. Certified translations of the documents must be provided if they are not in English or Irish. A decision upon an application for enforcement will usually be given within one week of the hearing. If the order is granted, then the Master must also grant certain protective measures sought.

The decision on the application for enforcement is notified to the applicant in open court. The applicant must then bespeak a copy of the order which will be reduced into writing by the Master's Registrar. The applicant must serve the respondent personally with a copy of the Master's order and a Notice of Enforcement. Leave is not required to serve these documents outside the jurisdiction.

An appeal against the grant of an order must be to the High Court by Notice of Motion served upon the successful applicant. The High Court has the power to stay the proceedings if appeal has been lodged in the State of judgment. Alternatively, if the time for appeal has not yet expired, the High Court may specify the time within which such appeal should be lodged.

If the refusal to grant an enforcement order is to be appealed, the applicant has five weeks from perfection of the order to appeal to the High Court. Again, the appeal is founded upon a Notice of Motion, together with an affidavit establishing that the party against whom enforcement is sought has been notified of the appeal and the date thereof in sufficient time for him to arrange his defence, or that all necessary steps have been taken to this end.

Any further appeal must be to the Supreme Court and on a point of law only. Notice of appeal must be lodged within five weeks of the perfection of the order of the High Court. However, such an appeal is likely to cause substantial delay as there is a waiting time of approximately two years for appeals from the High Court to the Supreme Court unless the matter is urgent or of public importance.

There have been no reported Irish decisions on the impact of public policy under Article 27. The area in which this issue may most likely arise is where the judgment in question is ancillary to a foreign divorce or might be contrary to the stricter Irish stance on issues such as abortion and contraception. In the former case, rather than invoke public policy the court might turn to Article 27(4).

10.12. Italy. Italy has a well-developed process of "exequatur" for cases outside the Conventions. For judgments from contracting States there is a presumption of "exequatur" which can only be displaced on the grounds appearing in Articles 27 and 28 of the Conventions. Application is made *ex parte* to the Court of Appeal (Corto d'Appello). This process is an alternative, rather than a replacement, to the full action of "exequatur" initiated by writ of summons.

Notification of the decision on recognition or enforcement is either by mail or by service by court officials at the domicile of the applicant if in Italy or otherwise to his appointed legal representative.

Appeal against enforcement must be begun by a writ of summons and leads to an adversarial hearing. The party against whom judgment is to be enforced may move objections on the merit, but only such as have been discovered after the "exequatur" hearing.

When a decision is refused, the party concerned may appeal directly to the Corto d'Appello. Again the proceedings are adversarial, therefore the defendant is entitled to appear by his legal representative and be heard.

Decisions of the Corto d'Appello can be challenged on a point of law to the Court of Cassation.

Italian judges have a wide discretion in the application of the concept of public policy. However, there are no particular grounds which are identifiable as preventing the enforcement or recognition of the judgment under Articles 27(1) of the Conventions.

10.13. Luxembourg. Application is made to the President of the District Court (Tribunal d'Arrondissment). Essentially the procedure follows that set out in the Conventions without additional requirements. Under Article 546–3 of the Code of Civil Procedure the clerk of the court will notify the applicant's lawyer of the President's decision by registered mail. In practice it is usually handed over to the lawyer.

Appeal against a decision on recognition or enforcement must be served by a bailiff on the opposing party. The competent court is the Cour Supérieure de Justice. The procedure is written and both parties must submit their arguments in writing.

In accordance with the provisions of the Conventions, the final appeal is on points of law only.

There are no specific grounds of public policy upon which recognition or enforcement of a judgment would be refused under Article 27.

10.14. The Netherlands. The process for recognition or enforcement of a judgment begins with a petition to the President of the Court for the relevant district filed by a Procureur enrolled in that district. The applicant is notified of the court's decision by letter.

If the defendant decides to appeal the authorisation of enforcement, the appeal is to the Arrondissementsrechtbank (district court) and is begun by summons (Dagvaarding). In contrast an appeal against refusal of enforcement is begun by a petition filed by the Procureur with the Court of Appeal.

A final appeal on a point of law by way of review is to the Hoge Raad.

The only potential ground of public policy upon which a court might refuse recognition or enforcement for public policy reasons is a serious breach of the fundamental principles of Dutch law. However the Hoge Raad has made it clear that use of Article 27(1) is to be exceptional.

10.15. Norway. Under the Lugano Convention an application for the enforcement of a judgment should be made to the local Court of Execution and Enforcement (namsrett) having jurisdiction over the area in which enforcement is to take place. The application should be accompanied by the documentation set out in Articles 46 and 47 of the Convention. The court in question may request certified translations of these documents.

The court may only refuse enforcement on the grounds set out in Articles 27 and 28 of the Convention, assuming that the judgment to be enforced concerns matters covered under Article 1 of the Convention.

Appeals against decisions authorising or refusing enforcement should be submitted to the relevant Regional Court ("Lagmannsrett"). A further appeal may be brought before the Supreme Court ("Hoyesterett") subject to approval by the Appeals Division of the Supreme Court ("Hoyesteretts kjoeremalsutvalg") or, in some cases, before the Appeals Division itself.

10.16. Portugal. As between the contracting States to the Conventions, the recognition and enforcement of judgments is governed by the provisions of the Conventions. Outside the Conventions the necessary procedure for recognition and enforcement of judgments is set down in Articles 1094 *et seq.* of the Portuguese Code of Civil Procedure. Accordingly a judgment of a foreign court or arbitration tribunal in a civil or commercial matter must first be reviewed and confirmed by a Portuguese court. The court in question is the Tribunal de Relação (Court of Appeal) for the judicial district where the defendant is domiciled.

Review and confirmation of a foreign judgment generally only considers the formal validity of the judgment. It will not be a review on the merits. There must be no doubts as to the authenticity of the documents containing the foreign judgment. Such authenticity will be reviewed according to the law of the State of origin. Translations must be provided of the judgment, sworn and legalised before a Portuguese Consulate.

The judgment must be final in the sense that no ordinary appeal must lie against it under the law of the State of origin. Further, the judgment must have originated in a court with jurisdiction over the case according to the rules of Portuguese private international law governing jurisdiction. Allied to this, the action in which judgment is to be enforced must not be one in respect of which an action has already been brought before the Portuguese courts and which is pending or has been decided.

The defendant must have been properly served with notice of the claim against him originally unless the case is one in which Portuguese law would have dispensed with the need for initial service. Where the judgment to be enforced was obtained in default, service of originating process must have been in person.

If the judgment to be enforced is against a Portuguese national, the judgment must not offend against the rules of Portuguese private international law as to jurisdiction. In the event of a conflict, the process of review becomes one of merit and the court must verify whether the judgment conforms with Portuguese law.

Once a request for review has been filed, the defendant is notified and must file his objections within ten days. After the expiry of this period, the applicant has eight days to file a reply. Thereafter the parties and the "Ministério Publico" have ten days to enter their submissions.

Apart from a challenge on the merits as set out above, there are various other grounds upon which confirmation of a judgment can be challenged. These include:

(1) proof that the decision to be confirmed was granted following bribery, corruption or prevarication;
(2) the existence of a document unknown to the defendant, or use of which was unavailable to the defendant in the original proceedings, which would have altered the initial judgment in the defendant's favour;
(3) the judgment to be confirmed is one in conflict with an earlier judgment between the parties.

Appeal from the decision of the Tribunal da Relação is generally an appeal in "agravo". When there has been a decision on the merits, the appeal is in "revista".

A challenge to the recognition and enforcement of a judgment on its merits can be mounted on grounds of public policy. Such challenge may be on the principles of public order on the international plane, not merely the national order.

10.17. Spain. Spain's recent accession to the Conventions means that one should examine the position not only under the Conventions but also previously.

Prior to the Brussels Convention, foreign judgments would only be recognised if there was a binding international treaty with the country concerned or to the extent that the foreign country would recognise Spanish judgments. In addition the judgments had to have been the consequence of a private suit and the defendant must have been represented at the hearing. Further the object of the action must have been legal under Spanish law. The judgment instrument must have fulfilled the requirements as to authenticity in its country of origin and met the procedural requirements of Spanish law.

The actual process for recognition and enforcement would either have been set down in the international treaty or in the case of reciprocity be equivalent to the steps required in the foreign country. Otherwise one had to turn to the exequatur proceedings before the Supreme Court. A demand for recognition would be presented to the first section of the Supreme Court. The request would then have to be served upon the defendant and the Attorney General's office within nine business days. If the court rejected the request the matter was terminated. If the request was granted, a certificate to that effect would be issued by the Secretary of the Supreme Court. The court would issue a corresponding order to the judge of first instance of the place of domicile or to the judge of the place where judgment was to be enforced.

With the entry into force of the Brussels Convention and subsequently the Lugano Convention, the exequatur proceedings have been abolished for judgments issued by a court of a contracting State. The new procedure for recognition and enforcement relies upon the documents required under Articles 46 and 47 together with translations thereof and a power of attorney in favour of the Spanish procurator and abogado which is valid under the law of the country of the applicant. The application for enforcement is made to the Juzgado de Primera Instancia and appeals against the grant of authorisation or its refusal are to the Audencia Provincial.

The Conventions replace bilateral conventions between Spain and the following Countries: France (May 28, 1968); Italy (May 22, 1973) and the Federal Republic of Germany (November 14, 1983).

10.18. Sweden. An application for the enforcement of a judgment under the Lugano Convention should be made to the Court of Appeal located in Stockholm ("Svea Hovrätt"). The application should be accompanied by the documentation set out in Articles 46 and 47 of the Convention. The court may request translations of these documents by an authorised translator.

Appeals against decisions authorising or refusing enforcement are tried by Svea Hovrätt. The judgment then given by the Court of Appeal may be further appealed to the Supreme Court ("Högsta Domstolen").

10.19. Switzerland. A distinction has to be made between judgments for monetary claims ("money judgments") and judgments for non-monetary claims ("non-money judgments").

The enforcement of money judgments takes place in special debt collection proceedings which are governed by the Federal Law on Debt Collection and Bankruptcy (DCB). On the other hand, the enforcement of non-money judgments is governed entirely by cantonal law. The applicable provisions are usually to be found in the respective cantonal Civil Procedure Codes. Further, Article 25 of the Federal Act on Private International Law (PIL) contains a comprehensive set of rules which have governed the question of the enforcement of a foreign judgment since January 1, 1989, and which have to be applied by the cantonal judges and courts. As far as judgments from Member States of the Lugano Convention are concerned, the rules of the PIL will no longer be applicable since the Lugano Convention contains its own rules which are directly applicable in Switzerland.

10.19:1. Non-Money Judgments. The application for the enforcement of a non-money judgment has to be filed with the competent cantonal enforcement judge (Vollstreckungs- oder Exequaturrichter) (Art. 32, Convention). In the Canton of Zurich this is the single judge (Einzelrichter). Local competence rests with the single judge at the domicile of the defendant or at the place where the assets concerned are located.

Enforcement proceedings are conducted on an *ex parte* and summary basis.

The application must contain the names and addresses of the parties involved, the relief sought, as well as a short statement on the grounds and the applicable law. In the Canton of Zurich the application may also be filed orally. It must be accompanied by the documents required according to Articles 46 and 47 of the Convention. If these documents are not drafted in the language of the court (German; in other cantons the court language can also be French or Italian), certified translations have to be filed. Furthermore, a representative entitled to accept service of the judge's decision on behalf of the applicant has to be named (Art. 33, Convention). Usually, this will be the applicant's counsel.

When the single judge makes his *ex parte* decision on the enforceability of a foreign judgment, he also decides whether to impose any protective measures as well if these have been requested by the applicant (Art. 39 Convention). Enforcement must be denied if one of the reasons listed in Articles 27 and 28 of the Convention applies.

Service of the decision on both parties is effected in the usual way (in the first instance by post with special acknowledgment of receipt; if this is not possible, by a bailiff or the police; through the Federal Office for Police Matters if the defendant lives abroad).

The defendant has one month from the moment of service in which to lodge an appeal with the competent cantonal high court, two months if he lives abroad. Pending the expiry of the time for appeal, and if an appeal is lodged, pending appellate proceedings, enforcement is stayed. If enforcement is denied, the applicant may lodge an appeal with the competent cantonal high court (Art. 40, Convention).

Appellate proceedings are *inter-partes* proceedings (Art. 37, Convention) and the appellate Court has full power of review. In the Canton of Zurich the "Rekurs" is the appropriate means of appeal pursuant to a Circular from the Cantonal High Court.

It is possible to appeal the decision of the Cantonal High Court to the Federal Supreme Court (Art. 37, paras. 2, 41, Convention). Enforcement is only stayed pending the appeal to the Federal Supreme Court upon special request and if the defendant persuades the court that otherwise he would suffer irremediable damage.

10.19:2. Money Judgments. As far as money judgments are concerned, there are some inconsistences between the provisions of the Convention and the DCB.

As already stated, money judgments are enforced under the rules of the DCB. Proceedings are initiated by a petition to the locally competent debt collection office which then issues and serves on the debtor a payment order, summoning the debtor to pay the sum due within 20 days or to lodge an opposition (Rechts-vorschlag) with the debt collection office within 10 days after service of the payment order. If the debtor raises an opposition, the creditor has to obtain the "lifting" of the opposition in special summary proceedings. The lifting of the opposition will be granted on the strength of an enforceable judgment. In the case of foreign judgments, the question of enforceability is dealt with as a preliminary question in the summary proceedings. Article 32, para. 1 of the Convention states that the application for the enforcement of a money judgment has to be addressed to the competent judge in the summary proceedings for the lifting of the opposition according to the DCB.

Now, contrary to the procedure according to the Lugano Convention (which provides for the decision on the recognition and enforcement of a foreign judgment to take place in *ex parte* proceedings in the first instance), the proceedings under the DCB are *inter partes* proceedings. Further, contrary to Article 39 of the Convention no provisional measures for the protection of the creditor's enforcement interests are possible.

The majority of the jurisprudential doctrine in Switzerland takes the view that the judgment creditor should be left with the choice to either initiate debt collection proceedings according to the DCB from the beginning, thereby waiving the surprise effect of *ex parte* proceedings and the possibility of protective measures pending appellate proceedings, or seek a decision on the enforceability of his judgment as a first step using proceedings under the Convention (*i.e. ex parte* and with the possibility of protective measures according to Article 39 of the Convention).

There is a further controversy as to which protective measures should be applied within the framework of Article 39 of the Convention. Some authors (including the High Court of the Canton of Zurich) are of the opinion that a decision on the enforceability of a foreign judgment should be considered a further ground for granting an attachment pursuant to Article 271 of the DCB. Others think that a provisional seizure of the debtor's assets should take place. No court rulings exist as yet.

CHAPTER 11

THE ENFORCEMENT AND EXECUTION OF JUDGMENTS

11.01. Introduction. Any judgment remains no more than a piece of paper unless the machinery to enforce it is in place. The Conventions provide the means to ensure, for example, that an Italian judgment once registered in Spain will work as well there as a Spanish judgment. What the Conventions do not attempt is to create a uniform basis of enforcement so that one must look to the domestic systems in each contracting State to assess the range of possibilities.

11.02. England and Wales. Generally the same remedies are available in the High Court and the County Court save that attachment of earnings orders in respect of ordinary money judgments are only available in the County Court.

11.02:1. Enforcement of Judgments or Orders to do or abstain from doing any Act. In both the High Court and the County Court such orders can be enforced by writ of sequestration or an order for committal. Where the judgment or order being enforced requires an act to be done, it must specify a time within which the act is to be done.

Before an order can be enforced in the manner described above, it must be served personally on the person to whom it is addressed. The order must further be indorsed with a penal notice to the effect that disobedience to the order will be liable to the process of execution.

11.02:2. Enforcement of Money Judgments. In the High Court money judgments can be enforced by the following methods:

(1) writ of *fieri facias*;
(2) charging order;
(3) appointment of a receiver;
(4) in cases as described above, committal or writ of sequestration;

(5) bankruptcy of an individual or partnership;
(6) winding up of a company.

The County Court equivalent to a writ of *fieri facias* is the warrant of execution. Where it is sought to enforce the judgment by this method there are certain jurisdictional limits to be observed. Enforcement of judgment debts greater than £5,000.00 must be in the High Court and of debts less than £2,000.00 in the County Court. The High Court only has power to make a charging order where the judgment debt is greater than £5,000.00.

11.02:3. Enforcement of Judgments for the Possession of Land. In the High Court a judgment for the possession of land may be enforced by:

(1) writ of possession;
(2) in appropriate cases an order for committal or a writ of sequestration.

Where the judgment creditor is seeking certain types of relief in the County Court, the application must be made in the court in which the judgment debtor resides or carries on business. The types of order concerned are (a) an oral examination; (b) a charging order; (c) an attachment of earnings order; or (d) a judgment summons. An oral examination affords the judgment creditor the means to examine the financial standing of the judgment debtor with the assistance of the court.

11.02:4. The Writ of *Fieri Facias* and the Warrant of Execution. The writ of *fieri facias* and the warrant of execution are the court's remedies for enforcement of a judgment against a debtor's goods. Where execution is sought through the High Court, the sheriff (or in the County Court, the bailiff) will enter the premises of the judgment debtor and seize sufficient goods to cover the debt and execution expenses. In the absence of a stay of execution or payment of the money owed, the sheriff or bailiff sells the goods by public auction.

A sheriff is independent of the court, whereas a bailiff is an official of the court. Unlike bailiffs, sheriffs are remunerated from the money they are able to recover. For this reason sheriffs may be more successful in recovering a judgment debt than bailiffs.

Excluded from the process of execution are tools, books, vehicles and other items of equipment necessary to a person for his personal use in his employment, business or vocation, together with such clothing, bedding, furniture, household equipment and provisions as are necessary for satisfying the basic domestic need of that person and his family. Also exempted from the warrant of execution are any money, banknotes, bills of exchange, promissory notes, bonds, specialities or securities for money belonging to the judgment debtor.

11.02:5. Writs/Warrants of Delivery. Such a warrant is the means of enforcing a judgment for the delivery of goods. A warrant for specific delivery provides for the delivery of the goods specified and payment of consequential damages. A warrant for delivery directs the seizure of the specified goods but gives the defendant the alternative of paying damages to the value of the goods.

11.02:6. Garnishee Proceedings. As a result of these proceedings debts due from a third party to the judgment debtor will be paid directly to the judgment creditor.

In the first instance a garnishee order is obtained *ex parte* binding the debt due from the third party until an *inter partes* hearing. At that hearing the third party may dispute whether such an order should be made absolute. Following an order being made absolute any payment by the third party to the judgment creditor is a valid discharge of liability to the judgment debtor.

11.02:7. Charging Order. A charging order secures the judgment debt against specified property of the judgment debtor. Such orders may lie against:

(1) a beneficial interest in land, government stock, stocks, shares, debentures and other corporate securities other than in a building society, funds in court;
(2) a beneficial interest under a trust;
(3) any interest held as a trustee if the interest is in an asset mentioned in head (1) above or under another trust and either the debtor was sued in his trustee capacity or the debtor is a bare trustee;

(4) interest and dividends payable on the above stocks, shares and funds in court.

In deciding whether to make such an order the court must have regard to the personal circumstances of the judgment debtor and also to whether making the order is likely to unduly to prejudice any other creditor of the debtor.

Charging orders follow a similar two-stage process as garnishee orders. An absolute order does not produce payment for the judgment creditor, it only imposes a charge against the particular property. Either the debtor will then pay voluntarily to have the charge removed or the judgment creditor will have to take separate sale proceedings.

11.02:8. Receivership Orders. The appointment of a receiver is only ordered by the court when no other legal method of enforcement is possible. The appointed receiver may be ordered to provide security by bond, guarantee or undertaking usually at twice the gross annual income of the property. Under the terms of the order the receiver is entitled to proper remuneration, must submit periodic accounts and pay money received into court as ordered.

11.02:9. Writ of Sequestration. The writ is addressed to four sequestrators and orders them to enter the premises of the person in contempt and to seize personal property until the contempt is discharged. In so far as the writ attaches to property, it should be registered as a charge on the land to protect the judgment creditor against subsequent purchasers.

11.03. Scotland. The following methods of enforcement are available, irrespective of whether the judgment being enforced emanated in the Court of Session or the Sheriff Court.

11.03:1. Service of a charge. A charge is a formal demand for payment, usually within 14 days. If not satisfied, the creditor may proceed to execute a poinding or commence bankruptcy or liquidation proceedings.

11.03:2. Poinding. This is a procedure by which a debtor's goods are seized. It is followed by a warrant sale, where the poinded goods are sold at public auction.

The Enforcement and Execution of Judgments

11.03:3. Inhibition. An inhibition is registered in a public register known as The Register of Inhibitions and Adjudications. It prevents the debtor from granting an unchallengeable title to a third party over any heritable estate owned by him at the date of the inhibition except with the consent of the inhibiting creditor. Likewise, the debtor cannot grant a good security over any such heritable estate. If a deed is granted in contravention of the inhibition (which in practice is rare) it may be set aside by the inhibiting creditor.

11.03:4. Arrestment. This freezes an obligation owed by the debtor by the person on whom the arrestment is served (the "arrestee"). Both corporeal moveables and incorporeal moveables, such as debts (including the defender's bank account) may be arrested. The arrestee is then prohibited from paying the debt, or delivering the goods arrested, to the debtor until the arrestment is recalled.

11.03:5. Furthcoming. Arrestment merely freezes the debt or goods as the case may be. An action of furthcoming is the means by which judicial authority is obtained to pay the debt to the arresting creditor.

11.03:6. Adjudication. A process whereby an inhibiting creditor may eventually obtain a real right over heritage owned by the debtor.

11.03:7. Earnings arrestment. This diligence requires the debtor's employer to deduct a prescribed amount each pay day and remit it to the creditor.

11.03:8. Sequestration. The means of making an individual or unincorporated body bankrupt.

11.03:9. Liquidation. *I.e.* the winding up of a company.

11.04. Austria. The primary means for enforcing monetary claims includes the attachment of salaries (Gehaltsexekution) and the seizure of property. An order for the attachment of a salary does not require knowledge of the employer's identity. Instead, the court will obtain the necessary data about the employment from the social security authorities. This data is then forwarded on to the plaintiff. The defendant's employer receives notice of the attachment order together with an order to transfer the sum to the plaintiff.

Should it not be possible to enforce a claim by an order for the attachment of a salary, application may be made to the court to seize the defendant's property. If it is not possible to attach the defendant's salary or seize his property, the defendant will be obliged to swear on oath as to his means.

Other procedures for the enforcement of a judgment would include the imposition of a charge over the defendant's immoveable property or the attachment of claims held by the defendant against third parties.

Where a judgment requires specific performance by the judgment debtor, execution of the judgment can be enforced either by monetary fines or by having the work carried out by a third party. In the latter case, the judgment debtor is obliged to pay the costs in advance. Collection of this payment may be the subject of separate enforcement proceedings.

11.05. Belgium. The form of execution in support of enforcement depends upon the nature of the property subject to execution.

Following a demand to pay served at least one day prior to attachment or garnishment, the judgment creditor may enforce against any tangible personal property, assets or chattels. However, the governing laws prescribe the property and level of income excluded from enforcement as being the minimum standard of living available to a person. Enforcement is carried out by a bailiff assisted by a witness and if necessary by a police officer.

Execution against real property also requires a prior demand for payment which must be registered with the Property Register. Following such a demand, the judgment creditor may enforce against all real property and accessories belonging to the judgment debtor. The judgment creditor may then request the "juge des saisies" to appoint a notary to supervise the sale of the property and distribution of the proceeds.

In the absence of prior agreement, a judgment creditor cannot enforce against a joint interest prior to the division thereof. The judgment creditor is entitled to participate in and initiate the division of the property.

If the judgment creditor has obtained an order for attachment prior to judgment on the merits, the process of execution is simplified. Judgment on the merits automatically converts the order for attachment into an order for execution. Consequently once a copy of the judgment is served upon the judgment debtor and it has become final, the judgment creditor may proceed directly with the sale of the judgment debtor's property.

11.06. Denmark. Where a judgment debtor has failed to comply with a judgment, the judgment creditor may approach the Sheriff's Court demanding the enforcement of judgment. The Sheriff's Court may make the order for execution subject to the provision of security by the judgment creditor.

Enforcement of a pecuniary claim is usually effected by way of execution levied upon the judgment debtor's assets and their subsequent sale, usually at the order of the court. If the claim to be enforced is not a pecuniary claim, the Sheriff's Court may enforce to the extent they can give a monetary value to the creditor's interest in having his claim enforced.

Execution cannot be levied before the time for compliance with the judgment has expired. However, the Sheriff's Court can waive this rule in special circumstances, for example, where there is a danger that the assets will be transferred out of the jurisdiction.

Distress can only be levied on assets belonging to the judgment debtor and not on those belonging to a third party, including the judgment debtor's wife or children. Further, it is not possible to distrain the judgment debtor's entire capital. The debtor is entitled to maintain a modest home and standard of living for his household. This exemption cannot be dispensed with by agreement between the parties. The word "household" encompasses not only spouses and children, but also other people with whom the judgment debtor is co-habiting.

The type of assets which may be distrained is also limited; excluded assets include those required for carrying on a profession or training and education. In this instance the right of the judgment creditor is to have a charge over such assets which protects his position against other creditors.

For those assets upon which distress is levied, sale is by public auction. Alternatively the Sheriff's Court may allow the judgment debtor a repayment scheme, in which case the assets distrained may not be removed from the judgment debtor.

11.07. Finland. In general, applications for enforcement are made to the bailiff by post. A request for enforcement should be made to the bailiff with jurisdiction over the relevant area, but he can transfer the matter *ex officio* to another bailiff if he is unable to perform the enforcement himself. The application to the bailiff must contain the relevant grounds for enforcement (*i.e.* final judgment) and, according to the nature of the case, any additional reports that are required for enforcement. The applicant may make the enforcement more effective by providing the bailiff with as accurate information as possible on the debtor and his funds. If an attorney submits the application, he has to have proper authorisation to do so.

The most important type of enforcement is distress, which is used when collecting a monetary debt or a debt consisting of goods. The debtor has the right to separate property that is essential for his livelihood, such as necessary tools, from the scope of the execution. The distrained property is converted into money usually by means of a compulsory auction. The most common form of enforcement is the attachment of the debtor's earnings. For social reasons, only a part of the earnings may be attached, and a sum that the debtor is considered to require for the support of himself and his family is excluded.

The enforcement by the bailiff may be appealed, in writing, to the executor-in-chief of the relevant provincial administration. The time period allowed for appeal to be lodged is 20 days. The decisions of the executor-in-chief may in turn be appealed (within 30 days) to the Court of Appeal and the decisions of the Court of Appeal on execution matters to the Supreme Court.

11.08. France. Two steps are essential to the enforcement of a judgment. First, the judgment must be notified to the judgment debtor. Generally this is carried out by the bailiffs (signification à parties). If the judgment has been given by the Tribunal de Grande Instance (TGI) notification must first be given to the judgment debtor's lawyer (signification à avocat), at least eight days before the notification by the bailiff. Judgments rendered by the Conseil des Prud'hommes or administrative courts are notified by the clerks of the courts and not by the parties.

The second stage of enforcement is entrusted to the bailiffs if payment is refused. The various measures possible for enforcement include:

(1) the seizure and sale of chattels (saisie-vente);
(2) the seizure and sale of immoveable property (saisie immobilière);
(3) garnishee orders and transfer of monies thus attached (saisie-attribution) (no judicial authorisation is required in addition to the judgment itself).

Any difficulties incidental to the execution process are within the jurisdiction of the judge of the TGI in charge of the enforcement proceedings (juge de l'exécution).

Since the summer of 1992 an order for saisie-attribution takes effect from the date of service, at which time, the claim or monies attached become the property of the judgment creditor notwithstanding any subsequent bankruptcy, judgment or attachment by another creditor. Prior to the summer of 1992, a saisie-arrêt (the predecessor of the saisie-attribution) became null and void if the debtor was placed in administration or forced into liquidation before the attachment was validated by a final judgment and later attachments entitled the creditors to share the monies attached by the first creditor.

11.09. **Germany.** The manner of enforcement will depend primarily upon the form of the judgment ordered by the court.

A money judgment may be executed by attachment of the judgment debtor's claims against third parties or by attachment and subsequent sale of moveable or tangible property. Alternatively execution may be enforced by levying execution against the judgment debtor's real property. Measures in support of such execution include judicial sale, the appointment of a receiver or administrator and, as a temporary measure, registration of a charge against the property to secure the debt.

When judgment is given for specific performance or a cease-and-desist judgment, the obligations imposed can be enforced either by requiring performance by the judgment debtor or, where it is reasonable and equitable, by a third party. Performance by a judgment debtor will be enforced by the possible imposition of a coercive fine or detention.

11.10. **Greece.** Under Greek law judgments and arbitral awards form part of the body of executive instruments for which the courts will provide their enforcement machinery. No enforcement proceedings are possible unless the claim is certain and final. Moreover, the quantity and quality of the subject-matter of the claim must be ascertainable from the executive instrument.

For claims other than monetary claims, various forms of executionary measures are possible depending upon the nature of the claim.

For a judgment for the delivery up of moveables, the bailiff removes and delivers the same to the judgment creditor. If the contested items are not in the debtor's possession he must swear an affidavit that he does not possess the moveables and does not know where they are. Where the claim is one for the delivery up of immoveable property, the bailiff will simply remove the debtor from possession.

If the effect of the judgment is that the judgment debtor is required to perform a certain act and this act can be done by a third party, the creditor is entitled to have the work done at the debtor's expense. Where performance is personal to the defendant, the court can oblige the debtor to perform the relevant acts by the imposition of a fine or imprisonment for up to a year in the event of non-compliance. Alternatively, if the claim is one to require the defendant to forbear from performing certain acts, the court may impose a fine or detention for up to a year for violation of the judgment.

Where the judgment requires a person to make a statement of will (*dilosis vouliseos*), that statement will be deemed to have been made upon the judgment becoming final.

Where a debtor refuses to satisfy monetary claims, the means of enforcement available are:

(1) the arrest and auction of assets belonging to the defendant whether in his possession or that of a third party;
(2) the forced administration of certain immoveable property or a business enterprise belonging to the debtor in order to satisfy the claim of the creditor;
(3) subject to certain conditions, the detention of the debtor in the debtor's prison for a period of up to one year.

If the assets of the debtor are insufficient to satisfy the judgment creditor's claim, the latter is entitled to petition the court to order the debtor to submit on oath a list of his assets, affirming that the list contains all his assets. A failure to provide the list may lead to detention in the debtor's prison and if the statement under oath is made but is untrue, the debtor is subject to the penalties for perjury.

The procedures for enforcement are not carried out by the court, but are conducted by the creditor under the supervision of the court. Since the procedures are both complex and formal, it is important to ensure strict compliance with the rules. Otherwise the enforcement proceedings may be invalidated leading to further delay.

The Enforcement and Execution of Judgments

Enforcement procedures are carried out by the bailiff and the auction officer, who is a notary public. On the instructions of the creditor, the bailiff will serve the demand for payment, conduct the arrest of the property or of the debtor and may if necessary call upon the police or other authorities to assist in the performance of his duties. He also assesses the value of the goods for auction and makes the arrangements for the auction including selecting the auction officer.

The auction officer is responsible for the conduct of the auction itself and for dealing with the post-auction issues. This will include accepting notification of the claims of the debtor's creditors and determining their priority *inter se*. Creditors have 15 days from the date of auction to submit their claims and supporting documentation. Upon completion of the auction and the payment of the auction price, the auction officer issues the summary of the report on auction and the document transferring title to the auctioned property to the highest bidder free of incumbrances and lien.

It is open to the debtor, or any third party showing lawful interest, to challenge the enforcement proceedings at all stages up to the auction. The challenge may be as to the validity of the judgment or other executive instrument or as to the conduct of the enforcement proceedings. Such defences are raised by way of Objections (Anakopi) either before the Court of Peace, if the judgment to be enforced is a judgment of that court, or, in all other cases, before the single-member Court of First Instance.

Objections to the validity of the judgment or the preparatory stages of the enforcement proceedings must be made within 15 days of the date of the first act in the procedure following the demand for payment, namely the arrest. Objections to the validity of enforcement acts following the arrest reports, or concerning the claim, must be brought up to the time of the last act in enforcement. Objections concerning the validity of the last enforcement act, the auction or re-auction, and adjudication must be brought within six months from the date of auction. For enforcement proceedings in respect of a monetary claim, the time period is shortened to 30 days if the auction is of moveables and 60 days if the subject-matter is immoveable property.

A debtor or third party objecting to the enforcement proceedings may bring a petition to have the auction suspended pending final judgment on the objections. A stay will only be granted, if in the court's opinion the enforcement proceedings will lead to irreparable damage to the objecting petitioner.

Alternative challenges to the enforcement proceedings may be mounted by the debtor either for correction of the auction programme or for an adjournment pending satisfaction of the creditor's claim. This last remedy is limited to an aggregate period of six months.

Even after the auction, the debtor may challenge the validity of the auction proceedings. If such a challenge is successful, the auction may be deemed to be cancelled and the relevant assets re-auctioned. Should an auction be cancelled, the highest bidder from the cancelled auction is entitled to the return of his purchase price in full if he is not the highest bidder at the re-auction.

Finally, the debtor or his creditors may challenge the list of creditors. This allows the single-member Court of First Instance to correct any potential mistakes of the auction officer in the application of the law concerning secured claims or the order of priority.

11.11. Ireland. There are various methods of execution available to a judgment creditor. These normally begin with the process of registration of judgment with the Judgments Office of the High Court. A consequence of registration is the publication of judgment in trade gazettes. The publicity attached to registration is often sufficient to force the judgment debtor to satisfy the judgment.

Apart from registration the court has other executory remedies open to a judgment creditor.

11.11:1. Execution Orders. The most common remedy for execution is to send the order for execution by the sheriff/county registrar. The sheriff/county registrar is empowered to seize all the debtor's moveable goods and may break into premises to seize the assets.

11.11:2. Enforcement of Court Orders Act 1926 and 1940. An application may be made to the district court calling upon the judgment debtor to file a statement of means and appear in court to support that statement, if necessary under examination.

If the court is satisfied that the defendant can pay the judgment debt, the district court will then make an order for the debt to be paid by instalments or in a lump sum. Failure to comply with this order enables the judgment creditor to apply to the court to have the judgment debtor committed to prison for his failure.

11.11:3. Order for Possession. This applies in respect of immoveable property and may be enforced by the sheriff who is requested to enter into the land and give possession of it to the judgment creditor.

11.11:4. Order for Delivery Up. If the judgment creditor obtains such an order it empowers the sheriff to enter the judgment debtor's premises and seize the assets listed in the order.

11.11:5. Garnishee. A garnishee order requires a third party to pay a debt owed to the judgment debtor to the judgment creditor. An application for this order has to be made to the Circuit or High Court.

11.11:6. Receiver by way of Equitable Mortgage. A garnishee order can only apply for the purposes of attaching an existing debt. If it is sought to attach future debts or periodic debts, an application should be made to the Circuit or High Court to appoint a receiver by way of equitable execution over the periodic payment or future debt. Such debts or payments will then be payable to the receiver and not to the judgment debtor.

11.11:7. Judgment Mortgage. If a judgment debtor owns land it is possible to register a judgment against the property as a judgment mortgage. The affidavit in support of the application is then registered against the land so that prospective purchasers are aware of the judgment debt.

A judgment creditor can initiate proceedings for the sale of the property. This is an extremely lengthy procedure and is usually only adopted where there are sufficient monies involved to make it worthwhile.

11.11:8. Bankruptcy. A cumbersome process, but one of which the threat alone may be sufficient. The procedure may be appropriate where the debtor has a substantial business but does not have debts which can be easily seized or realised.

11.11:9. Liquidation. Where the judgment debtor is a company, proceedings can be brought to have the company wound up. However, the costs of petition are substantial so that a petition should not be brought unless the judgment creditor is satisfied that the judgment debtor has sufficient assets to cover the costs of the petition and a dividend besides.

Apart from execution proceedings to enforce judgment, it is also possible to bring proceedings to locate and preserve the judgment debtor's assets pending execution. Orders for discovery are available in aid of execution as are Mareva Injunctions.

Normally interlocutory injunctions last only until judgment in the trial of the action. Accordingly, a separate application post-judgment will be necessary to ask the court to extend the injunction until satisfaction of judgment, or to grant an injunction if none existed previously.

There is some doubt that the court has the power to grant protective measures over assets in support of a judgment from a court of another contracting State until an enforcement order has been granted.

11.12. Italy. Where the judgment debtor fails voluntarily to comply with the judgment against him, the judgment creditor has to apply for execution to be levied. The judgment will be notified to the judgment debtor in the form of a certified true copy through the court. At the same time the judgment creditor serves the judgment debtor with an instrument of process known as a "precept". This requires the judgment debtor to perform his obligations within a certain time, not less than ten days from receipt, failing which the judgment creditor's judgment will be finally executed.

Where, despite the above, the judgment debtor continues to fail to comply with judgment, the judgment creditor may begin an action for execution. This phase is also regulated by the court and will result in a variety of measures. These include the following:

(1) The distraint of assets belonging to the judgment debtor whether in his possession or that of third parties: the creditor will then apply to the court for the distrained assets to be sold or assigned. After hearing the judgment debtor the judge will either order the assets sold by auction and the proceeds paid to the judgment creditor, or else, after appraising the value of the assets, assign them to the judgment creditor.

The Enforcement and Execution of Judgments 177

(2) The distraint of real property: the judgment debtor will be restrained by injunction from disposing of the assets and the charge will be registered in the property register. The court will establish a date of sale by public auction and the proceeds assigned to the judgment creditor.
(3) Where the judgment is for delivery-up of moveable or immoveable property, the court official can enforce compliance with the order and if necessary call for the aid of the law-enforcement bodies in support.
(4) The forced execution of judgments for specific performance or restraint of action.

11.13. Luxembourg. A copy of the judgment to be enforced must be served upon the judgment debtor. Thereafter the bailiff may attach any moveable goods which can then be sold at auction. Alternatively, the judgment may be attached to part of the judgment debtor's salary.

Execution is also possible by the registration of a charge against the judgment debtor's immoveable property and, if non-compliance with the judgment continues, sale of the property may follow.

11.14. The Netherlands. Upon the failure of a judgment debtor to pay a judgment debt voluntarily, the judgment creditor's advocate sends the enforceable copy of the judgment to a deurwaarder in the judgment debtor's locality. The deurwaarder serves the judgment on the debtor, and formally demands payment within two days. If the judgment is not satisfied within the two days, the deurwaarder may attach any assets in the possession of the judgment debtor. The assets may then be sold to satisfy the judgment. Attachment as a means of execution is known as an "executoriaal beslag" compared with attachment as a protective measure, "conservatoir beslag".

Assets belonging to the judgment debtor in the hands of third parties may also be attached. The judgment must first be served on the judgment debtor; the deurwaarder then attaches the assets in question by serving a document to that effect upon the third party, together with a copy of the judgment. There is then a time limit of eight days for the attachment to be served on the judgment debtor. The third party is obliged to declare the assets of the judgment debtor in his possession. The judgment debtor's earnings can be attached subject to a minimum amount reserved for basic living expenses.

If the judgment creditor has earlier obtained a conservatoir beslag final judgment automatically converts this to an executoriaal beslag.

For non-monetary judgments the form of enforcement orders depends on the subject matter of the action. Mandatory or prohibitive injunctions contain a clause providing for the payment of a fine (dwangsom) in the event of non-compliance. The fine may be either a lump sum or an amount calculated periodically for the duration of non-compliance. The fine is recoverable as a judgment debt. The dwangsom can only be cancelled, suspended or reduced if compliance with the order becomes impossible and then only from the date compliance becomes impossible.

Imprisonment on the order of the court is an alternative method of enforcing a judgment which is available in limited circumstances.

11.15. Norway. If a judgment debtor fails to comply with a judgment within the prescribed time limit, the judgment creditor may request the assistance of the local Commissioner for Execution and Enforcement ("namsmannen") responsible for the area in which the judgment debtor is domiciled.

Claims which are quantifiable in monetary terms may be enforced by the Commissioner granting the judgment creditor a legal charge over the assets of the judgment debtor. The charge may subsequently be enforced by means of the sale of the assets in question. Such sale will normally take place by public auction. However, the debtor is entitled to keep a certain minimum of personal assets.

Measures for the enforcement of non-pecuniary claims include:

(1) the forced transfer to the judgment creditor of the assets covered by the judgment; or
(2) the imposition of a fine payable for each day which elapses without the debtor handing over the assets to the creditor;
(3) if the asset in question is immoveable property, the Commissioner may evict the debtor and his personal belongings from the premises.

Finally, if the underlying judgment requires the debtor to take steps other than making a payment or handing over assets, the Commissioner may perform the activities on the debtor's behalf and at the debtor's cost or, alternatively, impose a fine payable for each day which elapses without the debtor fulfilling his obligations under the judgment.

11.16. Portugal. The procedure of execution is governed by Articles 801 *et seq.* of the Code of Civil Procedure (CCP). The enforcement machinery established by the Code provides for three forms of Order (art. 45, CCP).

11.16:1. Execution for the payment of a certain amount (articles 811 *et seq.*, CCP). The first phase of this procedure is the filing of the request for the notification of the debtor to pay, or to appoint goods to be attached. At this stage, the debtor can challenge the validity of the notice on appeal. Alternatively, the debtor may file an interplea which must be brought within ten days of the notification.

The second phase is the attachment of assets of the debtor. The law defines certain goods which cannot be attached, for example those necessary for the basic needs of the debtor, and other goods which can only be partially attached, for instance those goods necessary for the exercise of a profession.

The debtor is entitled to nominate the goods on which attachment should fall. He can only nominate choses in action in the absence of movable or immovable property. Separate sections of the CCP govern the attachment of movable goods, of immovable goods, and of choses in action.

Once the attachment is in place, the procedure moves to the convocation of the creditors and the assessment of their priority. Only the creditors who have rights *in rem* over the attached goods may claim payment through these proceedings. Both the plaintiff and the defendant may oppose the other creditors' claims. It is for the judge to decide which claims are to be recognised.

Finally payment may be levied by:

(1) the delivery of money — if the attachment has fallen on currency or cash deposits;
(2) the delivery up of certain of the attached goods;
(3) the assignment of income arising from certain attached property (usually immoveable property); or
(4) proceedings for the sale of the attached goods.

In specific cases, the sale will not be carried out through the court; for example in the instance of listed stock (sold on the stock exchange), goods of reduced value, (sold in certain cases through private negotiation), or private auctions when so required by the debtor and the creditors representing the majority of the creditors with priority rights over the goods to be sold.

More commonly, however, the sale will be carried out by the court, either by sealed bid or by public auction.

The day and time of the auction will be announced and the persons having preferential rights over the property will be specially notified.

11.16:2. Execution for the Delivery Up of a Specific Thing (Articles 928 *et seq.*, CCP). The plaintiff will request the notification of the debtor to deliver up the specific object within ten days. The defendant may oppose the court's notification, particularly if he has made improvements in the goods and wants compensation for them. If the debtor does not deliver the goods, delivery may be enforced by the court. If the property at issue is immoveable, the court will vest possession in the plaintiff.

11.16:3. Execution for Specific Performance (Articles 933 *et seq.*, CCP). This procedure is applicable when someone is obliged to render performance within a certain period and fails to do so. The creditor may request performance by another person or an indemnity for the damage. The debtor has ten days to object. The court will appoint experts to determine the cost of performance. Based on that valuation, the court will indicate goods of the debtor which will be attached to realise the cost of performance.

11.17. Spain. Ordinary enforcement procedures are generally applicable in respect of judgments rendered by domestic courts. In addition there are various forms of special enforcement procedure.

There are four different types of enforcement, depending on their purpose:

(1) expropriative enforcement (Ejecucion Expropiativa); intended to enforce an obligation to deliver any sum of money due under a judgment or other enforceable title;
(2) satisfactory enforcement (Ejecucion Satisfactiva); aimed at enforcing fulfilment of an obligation to deliver a specific

and concrete object;
(3) transformative enforcement (Ejecucion Transformativa); to enforce compliance with an obligation to do or not to do something;
(4) distributive enforcement (Ejecucion Distributiva); aimed at the universal enforcement of patrimony.

Jurisdiction over enforcement of a judgment rests with the court which passed judgment at first instance. The party which benefits from the judgment, or the holder of an interest in enforcement of the judgment, or the party liable may request enforcement proceedings.

When the judgment orders the doing or not doing of something, or the delivery of an object or a liquidated amount, then if such judgment is not fulfilled immediately, regardless of the cause, the creditor may seek an order for the seizure of property with a value sufficient to ensure satisfaction of the judgment with costs. The debtor can obtain release from the seizure by offering sufficient security.

Enforcement proceedings can be brought not only for satisfaction of judgments or court orders, but also in respect of other forms of title which are enforceable without the need for there to be a prior judgment. These forms of title are known as extrajudicial titles and include national or foreign arbitration awards recognised in Spain, demands in respect of legal fees, conciliation agreements, mortgage deeds and other forms of pledge which do not require forfeit of title.

11.17:1. Expropriative procedure. The procedure is begun upon the application of the party requesting payment, giving details of the title on which the application is based. The debtor's property may then be seized. After the property has been valued and sold at public auction the proceeds are transferred to the applicant.

From the time judgment is passed until its enforcement, the creditor is entitled to interest unless the debt is extinguished. If the debt is partially extinguished the court will determine the amount of interest payable.

Once an order has been made, the debtor's assets will be seized. If there is property specifically pledged or mortgaged to the debt, this property will be the first to be auctioned. In second rank, the order will fall upon money belonging to the debtor. Thereafter the order attaches to public effects and quoted securities followed by jewellery and negotiable credits, if any. Otherwise, or if these assets are insufficient to meet the debt, dividends of any nature; movable or semi-movable property; real estate; salaries or pensions; credits yet to mature; commercial and industrial premises will be sold.

A minimum salary, bedding, clothing, furnishings, books and instruments necessary for the exercise of the debtor's and his close relatives' professions are immune from seizure.

If the judgment orders payment of a liquidated amount, the debtor will be required to make settlement within a set period.

11.17:2. Satisfactory enforcement. The nature of an order ensuring the transfer of property will depend upon the subject-matter of the dispute. If the property at issue is immovable, the court will require it to be put at the disposal of the claimant. Moveable property must be immediately delivered to the claimant. If the property at issue is in the possession of a third party in good faith, the claimant will not be entitled to recover possession and must be satisfied with a remedy in damages from the debtor.

11.17:3. Transformative enforcement. If the judgment requires the respondent to perform certain obligations to the plaintiff and the respondent fails to do so, the plaintiff is entitled to have the obligations performed at the expense of the defendant. If this is not possible in the circumstances of the case, the court will substitute a right to damages instead. If the plaintiff's remedy is transferred to a remedy in damages, recovery can be pursued through expropriative enforcement.

Distributive enforcement. This form of enforcement is equivalent to bankruptcy procedures and is the only form of universal enforcement procedure for patrimony provided for in Spanish legislation.

11.18. Sweden. If a judgment debtor fails to comply with a judgment within the prescribed time limit, the creditor may request the assistance of the bailiff (Kronofogdemyndigheten). The application is normally made to the bailiff who is competent for the area where the judgment debtor is domiciled.

The enforcement of a monetary claim may be effected by legal distraint over the assets of the judgment debtor. The distraint may subsequently be followed up by means of a sale of the assets in question. The property, movable or immovable, can be sold at a public auction or through a private sale under the auspices of the authority of the bailiff.

A certain minimum of the debtor's assets, which are necessary for the debtor's personal use and trade, are not subject to distraint. For obligations which are not stated in monetary terms, the bailiff can order the debtor to take or to refrain from taking certain measures. A penalty notice may be attached to this order. The bailiff may also implement the necessary measures.

11.19. Switzerland. The methods of enforcement and execution of a judgment in Switzerland depend on the nature of the judgment. Money judgments are executed according to the provisions of the Federal Act on Debt Collection and Bankruptcy (DCB) which provides for (more or less) uniform proceedings in all Swiss cantons. The enforcement and execution of non-money judgments lie entirely with the cantons and is governed by the respective Civil Procedure Codes.

11.19:1. Money Judgments. Debt collection proceedings according to the DCB are started by a simple petition to the local Debt Collection Office (Betreibungsamt). The Debt Collection Office then issues a payment order and serves it on the debtor, summoning him either to pay the sum demanded by the creditor within 20 days or to enter an opposition against the payment order within 10 days. If an opposition is raised, debt collection proceedings are stayed and the creditor has to set aside the opposition, either by filing an action with the competent court or by way of summary proceedings in the event that the creditor already has a judgment or a written acknowledgment of the debt by the debtor.

In the Canton of Zurich summary proceedings take place before a single judge of the competent district court. On the strength of a final judgment, the judgment creditor can obtain the final lifting of the opposition and thereby the right to demand the continuation of the debt collection proceedings, either by way of seizure measures or by way of bankruptcy proceedings (depending on the debtor's status). In the summary proceedings the debtor can use only documentary evidence to establish that he has paid the debt, that payment of the debt has been deferred by the creditor, or that the claim is time-barred. Otherwise, the single judge will grant the final lifting of the opposition, provided the judgment is enforceable in Switzerland. He will decide on the enforceability of judgments emanating from foreign countries in the course of the summary proceedings (for details concerning judgments from Member States of the Lugano Convention, see Chapter 10, above).

Once the opposition has been lifted, the creditor must request the continuation of the execution procedure. If the debtor is an individual and not entered in the commercial register, the proceedings will continue with seizure measures and, later on, public sale of the debtor's property (as much as is necessary to satisfy the creditor's claim) in order to satisfy the creditor's claim. If the debtor is a corporate body or an individual entered in the commercial register, the proceedings will continue by way of bankruptcy, *i.e.* the debtor will have to be declared bankrupt by court order (in special proceedings) and all his assets will then form the estate in bankruptcy which will then be realised for the benefit of all the debtor's creditors and not only the one who initiated debt collection proceedings.

11.19:2. Non-Money Judgments. The execution of a non-money judgment which has been declared enforceable in Switzerland is governed by the provisions of the Civil Procedure Code of the canton where the execution has to take place. The judgment will be executed in the same way as a Swiss judgment.

In the Canton of Zurich the execution of non-money judgments is granted by the single judge of the competent district court during summary proceedings. Local competence rests with the court for the district where the debtor has his domicile, or where the property in dispute (moveable or immoveable) is located. If the debtor refuses to comply with the judgment, the Civil Procedure Code of the Canton of Zurich provides for various sanctions and remedies, such as the threat of imprisonment or a fine. An alternative, in the case of non-performance of a judgment for specific performance, is the threat that the act will be performed by a third party at the debtor's expense. Other measures include the application of compulsory measures against the debtor personally or against assets in his possession or, in the event that a personal statement of the debtor is needed (*i.e.* for an entry in the real estate register), the substitution of such a statement by a court order.

The single judge has full discretionary power to order the measures he deems appropriate and necessary in the specific case.

GLOSSARY

Action in Rem
Latin: action against a property, not a person.

Admiralty Actions
Disputes involving ships.

Adversarial Proceedings
This system involves the two advocates arguing against each other before the judge and differs from the Roman law inquisitorial system where the judge asks questions of the plaintiff and defendant.

Affiliation Proceedings
Court case to order the father of an illegitimate child to provide for the child's maintenance.

Ancillary Relief
Financial provision for adjustment of property rights ordered by a court for a spouse or child in divorce proceedings.

Appelate Court
Court with jurisdiction to hear appeals.

Attachment
Holding the debtor's property to prevent it from being sold until debts are paid.

Attachment of Earnings
Legal power to take money directly from a person's salary which is owed to the courts.

Bankrupt
Declared by a court as not capable of paying debts and as a consequence the bankrupt's affairs are put into the hands of a trustee.

Bare Trustee	A trustee whose role is negligible due to an active beneficiary.
Beneficial Interest	Interest of the beneficiary in a property or shares of a trust which allows occupation or an income from the property whilst ownership remains with a trustee.
Breach of Duty	Failing to do something which was agreed or is an obvious duty in tort.
Burden of Proof	Duty to prove something which has been alleged in court.
Capacity	Ability to enter into a legal contract, *i.e.* a person who is over 18 years old and of sound mind.
Cause of Action	Reason why a case is brought to court.
Charging Order	Order in favour of a judgment creditor granting him a charge over the debtor's property.
Chattels	Moveable property.
Collegiate (High Court)	A small group of people which represents the whole group.
Committal Order	Order sending someone to prison for contempt of court.
Consequential Damages	Compensation for the loss or harm suffered as a result of the illegal act committed.
Contempt of Court	Refusal to obey the order of a court.

Glossary

Contract	Legal agreement between two or more parties.
Counterclaim	The defendant claims against the plaintiff who has already brought a claim against him.
Court Action	Civil case where one person sues another in court.
Cross-undertaking	Promises by opposing sides to do something.
De Novo	Latin: starting again.
Declarative Hearing	Hearing in which something is merely declared, *i.e.* legal position of the various parties.
Deponent	Someone who makes a statement under oath or by affidavit.
Distrain	Verb: to seize goods to pay for debts.
Distress	Goods belonging to the debtor which are taken to pay for the debts.
Domicile	Country where someone is deemed to live permanently or where a company's office is registered.
Equitable Powers	A court's inherent powers under the laws of equity to implement a fair and just judgment.
***Ex Parte* Proceedings**	Latin: meaning on behalf of *i.e.* an application made to a court where only one side is represented and no notice is given to the other side (often where the application is for an injunction).

Fraud	Harming someone by obtaining property or money from him after making him believe something which is not true or an act of deceiving someone in order to make money.
Hearsay Evidence	Evidence given by a witness who did not witness the act himself but heard about it from another source.
Injunction	Court order compelling someone to stop doing something or not to do something.
In Personam	Latin: meaning against a person.
Intellectual Property	Ownership of something which is intangible, *i.e.* a copyright or patent or design.
Interlocutory Injunction	Injunction granted which remains in force until the case comes to court.
Interlocutory Judgment	Judgment given during the action but before the full trial.
Interlocutory Proceedings	Taking place before the full trial.
Interpleader	Court action started by a person who has property which is not his but is claimed by two or more people or by a person who may be sued by two different parties.
Intervener	Someone who intervenes in an action to which he was not originally a party.

Glossary

Joint Interest	Ownership of shares or property held by two or more people.
Judgment	Decision of the court.
Judgment in Default	Judgment against a defendant who fails to defend his case.
Legal Professional Privilege	Correspondence between client and legal adviser which is protected against disclosure during legal proceedings.
Lien	A legal right to keep someone's goods until a debt has been paid.
Limitation Period	Time limit in which to start legal proceedings (usually six years).
Liquidated Damages	Specific amount calculated as loss suffered.
Liquidation	A company may be wound up or closed down and its assets sold.
Locus Delicti	Latin: meaning the place where the event occurred.
Mandatory Injunction	A court order compelling someone to do something.
Merits of the Case	Main question which is at issue in an action.
Motion	Application to a judge in court asking for an order in favour of the person making the application.
Natural Justice	The concept of a fair judgment which does not follow the strict reading of the law but reaches a conclusion which accords with society's view of what is true and fair.

Notarial Deed	Deed validated by a notary who is a lawyer with the authority to witness and draw up certain documents making them official.
Patent	Official document showing that a person has the exclusive right to make and sell an invention. Verb to patent: to register an invention. Adjective: obvious or clear to see.
Petition	Written application to the court asking for the court to do something, *i.e.* make an order.
Pleadings	Document setting out the claim of the plaintiff or the defence of the defendant or giving the arguments which the two sides will use in the proceedings.
Private Suit	Civil legal action brought on by a private person not by a public authority.
Probate Action	Dispute involving a will.
Process of Leap Frog	Instead of following the usual system of appeal from one court to another, the Court of Appeal stage is missed out and the point of law goes directly to the House of Lords.
Public Policy	The concept of the public good which may cause a judgment to be made which goes against the general trend of decisions or obvious conclusion.

Glossary

Ratify	Approve officially something which has already been agreed unofficially so making it legally binding.
Registered Title	Title to land which has been registered with the Land Registry.
Rejoinder	Pleading served in answer to a plaintiff's reply.
Reply	Written statement by a plaintiff in a civil case in answer to the defendant's defence.
Representative *Ad Litem*	The applicant appoints a representative on whom documents addressed to the applicant may be served in that jurisdiction, *i.e.* when the applicant lives abroad.
Res Judicata	Latin: meaning matter on which a judgment has been given.
Rescind	To cancel an agreement.
Security for Costs	Guarantee that one of the parties in a dispute will pay costs (money may be deposited as security for the defendant's costs).
Service	Delivery of a document such as a writ or summons to someone or to his solicitor, *i.e.* to acknowledge service: to confirm that a legal document such as a writ has been received.
Set Aside	At a later hearing of the case the court decides not to apply the earlier decision.

Stay	Temporary stopping of an order made by a court.
Strike Out	To cancel an action which has started, because the plaintiff has not appeared or for some other reason.
Subpoena	Court order to appear in court.
Summary Proceedings	Proceedings which result in an immediate judgment of a case applied for by a plaintiff who believes the defendant cannot put forward any sensible defence.
Summons	Official command from a court requiring someone to appear in court to be tried for a criminal offence or to defend a civil action.
Summons *Inter Partes*	Latin: a summons by one party on another.
Third Party Proceedings	Introduction of anyone who is not one of the two main parties in the proceedings by the defendant.
Tort	Civil wrong done by one person to another and entitling the victim to claim damages.
Trust	A fiduciary position of holding property for the benefit of another.
Unconditional Appearance to Proceedings	To register with a court that a defendant intends to defend an action.
Undertaking	A legally binding promise.

Viva Voce	Latin: meaning orally or by speaking.
Void	Not legally valid.
Writ of *Fieri Facias*	Usually a writ which is a court order to a sheriff telling him to seize goods of a debtor against whom judgment has been made.
Writ of Sequestration	A writ served on someone which allows the seizure of property on the court's order often where the defendant is guilty of contempt of court.

INDEX

Adjudication,
  Scotland, 11.03:6
Anton Piller Order, 5.02
Arrestment, 11.03:4

Bankruptcy,
  Ireland, 11.11:8
Brussels and Lugano Conventions,
    1.01–1.25
  ancillary measures, 1.05
  Austria, 1.10
  basic jurisdiction, 1.03
  Belgium, 1.11
  consumer contracts, 1.04:4
  Denmark, 1.12
  exclusive jurisdiction, 1.04:2
  Finland, 1.13
  France, 1.14
  Germany, 1.15
  Greece, 1.16
  implementation, 1.08–1.25
  insurance claims, 1.04:4
  interpretation, 1.07
  Ireland, 1.17
  Italy, 1.18
  jurisdiction by agreement, 1.04:3
  Luxembourg, 1.19
  Netherlands, 1.20
  Norway, 1.21
  Portugal, 1.22
  recognition and enforcement of
    judgments, 1.06
  scheme, 1.02
  scope, 1.02
  Spain, 1.23
  special jurisdiction, 1.04:1
  Sweden, 1.24
  Switzerland, 1.25
  United Kingdom, 1.09

Charging order, 11.02:7
Conduct of proceedings, 4.01–4.19:3.
  See also Pre trial preparation.
Costs,
  security for. *See* Security for costs.
Court structure, 2.01–2.19
  Austria, 2.04

Court structure—*cont.*
  Belgium, 2.05
  Denmark, 2.06
  England and Wales, 2.02
  Finland, 2.07
  France, 2.08
  Germany, 2.09
  Greece, 2.10
  Ireland, 2.11
  Italy, 2.12
  Luxembourg, 2.13
  Netherlands, 2.14
  Norway, 2.15
  Portugal, 2.16
  Spain, 2.17
  Sweden, 2.18
  Switzerland, 2.19
    cantonal commercial court, 2.19:5
    cantonal Court of Cassation,
      2.19:7
    Cantonal High Court, 2.19:6
    district courts, 2.19:2
    labour courts, 2.19:3
    lease courts, 2.19:4
    single judges, 2.19:1
    Swiss Federal Supreme Court,
      2.19:8
  Scotland, 2.03

Domicile, 7.01–7.19
  Austria, 7.04
  Belgium, 7.05
  Denmark, 7.06
  England and Wales, 7.02
    bodies corporate, 7.02:2
    natural persons, 7.02:1
    trusts, 7.02:3
  Finland, 7.07
  France, 7.08
  Germany, 7.09
  Greece, 7.10
  Ireland, 7.11
  Italy, 7.12
  Luxembourg, 7.13
  Netherlands, 7.14
  Norway, 7.15
  Portugal, 7.16
  Scotland, 7.03

Domicile—*cont.*
  Spain, 7.17
  Sweden, 7.18
  Switzerland, 7.19

Earnings arrestment, 11.03:7
Enforcement and execution of
  judgments, 11.01–11.19
  Austria, 11.04
  Belgium, 11.05
  Denmark, 11.06
  England and Wales, 11.02
    charging order, 11.02:7
    fieri facias, 11.02:4
    garnishee proceedings, 11.02:6
    judgments or orders to do or
      abstain from doing act,
      11.02:1
    money judgments, 11.02:2
    possession of land, 11.02:3
    receivership orders, 11.02:8
    warrant of execution, 11.02:4
    warrants of delivery, 11.02:5
    writ of sequestration, 11.02:9
  Finland, 11.07
  France, 11.08
  Germany, 11.09
  Greece, 11.10
  Ireland, 11.11
    bankruptcy, 11.11:8
    enforcement of Court Orders Act
      1926 and 1940, 11.11:2
    execution orders, 11.11:1
    garnishee order, 11.11:5
    judgment mortgage, 11.11:7
    liquidation, 11.11:9
    order for delivery up, 11.11:4
    order for possession, 11.11:3
    receiver by way of equitable
      mortgage, 11.11:6
  Luxembourg, 11.13
  Netherlands, 11.14
  Norway, 11.15
  Portugal, 11.6
    delivery up of specific thing,
      11.16:2
    payment of specific amount,
      11.16:1
    specific performance, 11.16:3
  Scotland, 11.03
    adjudication, 11.03:6
    arrestment, 11.03:4
    earnings arrestment, 11.03:7
    forthcoming, 11.03:5

Enforcement and execution of
  judgments—*cont.*
  Scotland—*cont.*
    inhibition, 11.03:3
    liquidation, 11.03:9
    poinding, 11.03:2
    service of charge, 11.03:1
    sequestration, 11.03:8
  Spain, 11.17
    expropriative procedure, 11.17:1
    satisfactory enforcement, 11.17:2
  Sweden, 11.18
  Switzerland, 11.19
    money judgments, 11.19:1
    non-money judgments, 11.19:2
Establishment of jurisdiction,
  6.01–6.19
  Austria, 6.04
  Belgium, 6.05
  Denmark, 6.06
  England and Wales, 6.02
  Finland, 6.07
  France, 6.08
  Germany, 6.09
  Greece, 6.10
  Ireland, 6.11
  Italy, 6.12
  Luxembourg, 6.13
  Netherlands, 6.14
  Norway, 6.15
  Portugal, 6.16
  Spain, 6.17
  Scotland, 6.03
  Sweden, 6.18
  Switzerland, 6.19
  PIL, 6.19
Execution of judgments. *See*
  Enforcement and execution of
  judgments.

Fieri facias, 11.02:4
Foreign originating process,
  service of. *See* Service of foreign
  originating process.
Furthcoming, 11.03:5

Garnishee order,
  Ireland, 11.11:5
Garnishee proceedings, 11.02:6

Inhibition, 11.03:3
Interim protection of assets pending
  trial, 5.01–5.19:4

Index

Interim protection of assets pending trial—*cont.*
  Austria, 5.04
  Belgium, 5.05
  Denmark, 5.06
  England and Wales, 5.02
  Finland, 5.07
  France, 5.08
    attachment, 5.08
  Germany, 5.09
    attachment orders, 5.09:1
    temporary injunctions, 5.09:2
  Greece, 5.10
    judicial sequestration, 5.10:4
    prenotation of mortgage, 5.10:1
    provisional accommodation, 5.10:3
    public deposit, 5.10:5
    revocation of provisional measures, 5.10:6
    saisie conservatoire, 5.10:2
  Ireland, 5.11
  Italy, 5.12
  Luxembourg, 5.13
  Netherlands, 5.14
  Norway, 5.15
  Portugal, 5.16
    enrolment, 5.16:5
    injunctions, 5.16:6
    interim delivery up, 5.16:1
    suspension of corporate decisions, 5.16:2
    suspension of new works, 5.16:4
  Scotland, 5.03
  Spain, 5.17
  Sweden, 5.18
  Switzerland, 5.19
    monetary claim, 5.19:4
    non-monetary claim, 5.19:3
    procedure, 5.19:2
    provisional measures, 5.19:1

Judgment mortgage,
  Ireland, 11.11:7

Liquidation,
  Ireland, 11.11:9
  Scotland, 11.03:9
Lugano Convention. *See* Brussels and Lugano Conventions.

Order for delivery up,
  Ireland, 11.11:4

Originating process for civil litigation, 3.01–3.19
  Austria, 3.04
  Belgium, 3.05
  Denmark, 3.06
  England and Wales, 3.02
  Finland, 3.07
  France, 3.08
  Germany, 3.09
  Greece, 3.10
  Ireland, 3.11
  Italy, 3.12
    cognizance proceedings, 3.12:1
    enforcement procedure, 3.12:2
    special process, 3.12:3
  Luxembourg, 3.13
  Netherlands, 3.14
  Norway, 3.15
  Portugal, 3.16
  Scotland, 3.03
  Spain, 3.17
  Sweden, 3.18
  Switzerland, 3.19
    ordinary proceedings, 3.19:1
    summary proceedings, 3.19:2

Poinding, 11.03:2
Pre trial preparation, 4.01–4.19:3
  Austria, 4.04
  Belgium, 4.05
  Denmark, 4.06
  discovery, 4.02
  England and Wales, 4.02
  exchange of pleadings, 4.02
  Finland, 4.07
  France, 4.08
  Germany, 4.09
  Greece, 4.10
  interlocutory injunctive relief, 4.02
  interrogatories, 4.02
  Ireland, 4.11
  Italy, 4.12
  Luxembourg, 4.13
  Netherlands, 4.14
  Norway, 4.15
  payment into court, 4.02
  Portugal, 4.16
  scope for gathering evidence, 4.01
  Scotland, 4.03
    interim orders, 4.03
    Specification for Recovery of Documents, 4.03
  Spain, 4.17
  Sweden, 4.18

Pre trial preparation—*cont.*
  Switzerland, 4.19
    decision-making phase, 4.19:3
    discovery phase, 4.19:2
    introductory phase, 4.19:1

Receiver,
  by way of equitable mortgage, Ireland, 11.11:6
Receivership orders, 11.02:8
Recognition and enforcement of judgments, 10.01–10.19
  applications, 10.01
  Austria, 10.04
  Belgium, 10.05
  Denmark, 10.06
  England and Wales, 10.02
  Finland, 10.07
  France, 10.08
  Germany, 10.09
  Greece, 10.10
  Ireland, 10.11
  Italy, 10.12
  Luxembourg, 10.13
  Netherlands, 10.14
  Norway, 10.15
  Portugal, 10.16
  Scotland, 10.03
    contracting states under Conventions, 10.03:1
    England and Wales, 10.03:2
    judgments of courts of countries not party to Convention, 10.03:3
    judgments outwith scope of Conventions, 10.03:3
    money judgments, 10.03:2
    non-money judgments, 10.03:2
    Northern Ireland, 10.03:2
  Spain, 10.17
  Sweden, 10.18
  Switzerland, 10.19
    money judgments, 10.19:2
    non-money judgments, 10.19:1

Security for costs, 9.01–9.19
  Austria, 9.04

Security for costs—*cont.*
  Belgium, 9.05
  Denmark, 9.06
  England and Wales, 9.02
  Finland, 9.07
  France, 9.08
  Germany, 9.09
  Greece, 9.10
  Ireland, 9.11
  Italy, 9.12
  Luxembourg, 9.13
  Netherlands, 9.14
  Norway, 9.15
  Portugal, 9.16
  Scotland, 9.03
  Spain, 9.17
  Sweden, 9.18
  Switzerland, 9.19
Service of foreign originating process, 8.01–8.19
  Austria, 8.04
  Belgium, 8.05
  Denmark, 8.06
  England and Wales, 8.02
  Finland, 8.07
  France, 8.08
  Germany, 8.09
  Greece, 8.10
  Ireland, 8.11
  Italy, 8.12
  Luxembourg, 8.13
  Netherlands, 8.14
  Norway, 8.15
  Portugal, 8.16
  Scotland, 8.03
  Spain, 8.17
  Sweden, 8.18
  Switzerland, 8.19
Sequestration, writ of, 11.02:9, 11.03:8
Specific performance,
  Portugal, 11.16:3

Trial,
  England and Wales, 4.02

Warrant of execution, 11.02:4
Warrants of delivery, 11.01:5

WITHDRAWN FROM UNIVERSITY OF PLYMOUTH LIBRARY SERVICES

90 0339410 9

Science

SEVEN DAY LOAN 24 JUN 2002

This book is to be returned on or before the date stamped below

2 0 NOV 2002

2 2 NOV 2002

UNIVERSITY OF PLYMOUTH

PLYMOUTH LIBRARY

Tel: (01752) 232323

This book is subject to recall if required by another reader
Books may be renewed by phone
CHARGES WILL BE MADE FOR OVERDUE BOOKS